Global Potluck

Jenif Niem

JENNIFER NIEMUR

Order this book online at www.trafford.com/08-1114
or email orders@trafford.com

Most Trafford titles are also available at major online book retailers.

Note for Librarians: A cataloguing record for this book is available from Library
and Archives Canada at www.collectionscanada.ca/amicus/index-e.html

Printed in Victoria, BC, Canada.

ISBN: 978-1-4251-8610-4

*We at Trafford believe that it is the responsibility of us all, as both individuals and corporations,
to make choices that are environmentally and socially sound. You, in turn, are supporting this
responsible conduct each time you purchase a Trafford book, or make use of our publishing services.
To find out how you are helping, please visit www.trafford.com/responsiblepublishing.html*

*Our mission is to efficiently provide the world's finest, most comprehensive book publishing
service, enabling every author to experience success. To find out how to publish your book, your
way, and have it available worldwide, visit us online at www.trafford.com/10510*

Trafford PUBLISHING® www.trafford.com

North America & international
toll-free: 1 888 232 4444 (USA & Canada)
phone: 250 383 6864 ♦ fax: 250 383 6804 ♦ email: info@trafford.com

The United Kingdom & Europe
phone: +44 (0)1865 487 395 ♦ local rate: 0845 230 9601
facsimile: +44 (0)1865 481 507 ♦ email: info.uk@trafford.com

10 9 8 7 6 5 4 3

Global Potluck

Acknowledgments

I would like to thank my husband Adam for his moral and financial support. I would also like to acknowledge Heifer International for doing the right thing and doing it so well, so the rest of us can feel good about the contributions we make.

Finally, this cookbook could not have been completed without the assistance of all the recipe contributors:

Sheryl Tusch (Mom gets top billing!)
Michelle Alster
Sandra Anderson
Portia Boss
Ruth Boss
Jerry Bronkema
Shawn Cole
Geralyn Coleman
Gloria DeKleine
Vinita Dowd
Luarna Duncan
Steve Gillich
Beth Heckman
Karleen Holm

Tannis Kateca
Maria Los
Cindy Loza
Lisa Maloney
Teri Mercier
Iris Myaard
Linda Abenante O'Donoghue
Noemi Cervantes Raeside
Julie Rohrer
Renee Schab
Dee Tusch
Linda Van Dam
Sandra Van Dam

Introduction

To learn about global cuisine is to follow the migration of peoples across the planet, over centuries, and to enjoy the mingling of cuisines in their wake. It was only a few short years ago that "fusion cuisine" became a trend, but since that time it has appeared in menus and cookbooks everywhere. Ironic, really, since fusion cuisine is nothing new: when you bite into a bowl of spaghetti with tomato sauce, you are sampling noodles from China (who learned the process of milling grains from Middle Eastern traders), tomatoes from the Americas, and herbs and spices from Europe and Asia. It's not just ingredients that have been blended together over the centuries, but our vocabulary too: another example of culinary cross-pollination is the word gourmet, which we all associate with French cooking. It actually comes from the Farsi word *gormeh* (stew). The term was likely picked up during the medieval crusades, when French soldiers witnessed the lavish meals produced by their Muslim counterparts.

The development of different world cuisines offers a fascinating look at how people – and in turn, foods and cooking techniques, have traveled across the globe. The exchange of foodstuffs between Europe and the Americas, often referred to now as the "Columbian Exchange," had a massive impact on our history. In his book *Near a Thousand Tables*, Felipe Fernández-Armestu asserts that "it remains unquestionable that the great ocean-borne exchange of biota of the last five hundred years constituted the biggest human intervention in environmental history since the beginnings of species domestication." Italian pasta sauce, Swiss chocolate, English shepherd's pie, and spicy Thai and Indian food – none of these would have been possible without the introduction of New World ingredients to other civilizations.

Two other phenomena impacted culinary history on a global scale: the slave trade between Europe, Africa, the Caribbean and the Americas, and the colonization of countries by foreign powers to feed Europe's demand for spices, rum, coffee, tea and other resources. Helen's may have been the face that launched a thousand ships, but centuries later it was the money to be made from these goods that brought the battling fleets of Portugal, England, Spain and the Netherlands out in full force. While these periods in history may be examples of the worst humans can do to one other, they did allow for a huge interchange of people across cultures. As a result, for just one small example, peanuts traveled from South America to Africa, then west again to the southern United States.

On a lighter note, exploration of global cuisine is a concept that lends itself well to sharing foods with friends and family, discovering new ingredients, enjoying the rich sounds of world music and imagining your next travel destination. A "potluck" is just such a gathering of loved ones, to share food and companionship. We've all had our share, although they usually include local, tried-and-true dishes, and not recipes from far-flung locales. Ché Guevara once said "Homesickness begins with food," and indeed, just imagining the potlucks I have attended (they are legion) resurrects fond memories of cheesy hash brown casseroles, Technicolor jello salads, and my great-aunts' custard pies, and makes me ache for the comfort of home.

In my own family, potlucks are not without their legends. There was the year my dear sister Cindy suffered second-degree burns in the car, after the scalloped potatoes slurped out of the crock-pot when Mom made a somewhat enthusiastic right turn on the way to an Yntema family potluck. And who can forget my neighbor Jeff, who, despite tornado warnings and a severe thunderstorm, held a weenie and marshmallow roast in his driveway because we had planned this barbeque and it was going to HAPPEN! I also have fond memories of our friend Randall waxing poetic with his friend John, as they did a riff as – I am not making this up - pirate neurosurgeons, while gobbling down potluck fare on the front steps of his Kalamazoo home ("...argh, I've done many a lobotomy in me day, argh..."). And years later, when Randall died, literally hundreds of people showed their love and compassion through food for weeks on end.

What I love about potlucks is this spirit of community, and how sharing our time, talents and material wealth comes so easily to us as soon as food is involved. It's like something magical happens and we suddenly become eager to share. We need that joy of giving: we crave it. And let's be honest, we crave the reviews, too. At least once in our lives we have all waited eagerly to gauge the reactions of those taste-testers.

Consider this book, then, to be its own potluck of sorts. While this group of family and friends might not be sharing *food* with you, they are sharing fabulous recipes, experiences, and stories. We, as a group, offer this Global Potluck to you to savor, curl up with at night, and stain the pages with tomato sauce and other spatterings as often as you like. As you read these recipes, consider the joy and inspiration that comes from sharing new foods and learning about other cultures. Consider hosting your own global potluck, and in doing so, if you want, you can even raise funds or awareness to support humanitarian aid in the countries that gave us these rich culinary traditions – in whatever way you feel is appropriate and meaningful. For my part, 80% of the profits from this book will be given to Heifer International.

As a newcomer to Canada, I was surprised to discover that Canadians refer to their citizenry as a "mosaic" as opposed to the American concept of the "melting pot." The mosaic concept reflects a coming-together of different cultures, without any one culture losing its unique identity and traditions. It is certainly a concept worth exploring, and how better to do that than with food?

Before we begin, then, a quick word about what this book is, and what it isn't. It is a collection of recipes from myself, friends, and family members, "peppered" if you will, with fun bits of food trivia and culinary history. Everyone who chipped in has their name by their recipe: if you do not see a name under the recipe, it's mine.

It is not a gourmet cookbook: all the recipes (with a few exceptions) can easily be made in any home kitchen without buying special equipment. Neither is it an exhaustive list of world cuisines: major contributors to global cuisine such as Japan, Korea, Israel and Portugal are missing due to various limiters on the parameters of this book, and each chapter that *is* included does not feature every single one of that country's major dishes. Finally, as you will see, it is not a strictly health-conscious cookbook – where possible, I have created healthy alternatives and eliminated trans fats, but let's face it, in the words of Robert Redford, "health food may be good for the conscience but Oreos taste a hell of a lot better."

One last aside before we get to the good stuff: since this cookbook was written partly in the U.S. and partly in Canada, I had to choose which side of the 49th parallel would win out in terms of measurements. So with apologies to my Canadian readers, all recipes use English measurements. For those used to metric, here are some quick rules of thumb: 5 ml is a teaspoon, 450-500 grams is close enough to a pound (it's 454 to be exact) and in America, icing sugar is called powdered sugar, and soya sauce is called soy sauce.

The Destination Potluck

Travel is the means by which we escape the ordinary and open our minds to new experiences, languages, cuisines, music, and art. Yet when we return from a trip, the food often becomes the most lasting memory of our journey. What were some of the highlights of your most recent trip? Was there a restaurant, roadside stand, or market that stands out? Try to recall those flavors, aromas and atmospheres, and have fun recreating them in the kitchen. It will be a five-senses trip down memory lane. One memory that stands out for me was a simple roadside stand on the way to Coral Bay on St. John, USVI. Vi operates her "Snack Shack" out of a miniscule clapboard building. To get any food, you have to step gingerly pass the goats and chickens in the front yard and holler for her. Her son would have been up earlier that morning, diving for conch that she serves up in her fritters. On the same trip to St. John, we downed cheeseburgers on a floating restaurant, converted from an old brigantine nestled in a cove off Norman Island (BVI), licking our fingers and watching the stingrays glide past as we listened to – you guessed it – Jimmy Buffett's *Cheeseburgers in Paradise*. I suppose cooking also takes the sting out of returning home from a vacation in paradise, because for months after that trip, I was dancing around the kitchen to reggae music, cooking everything with lime, cilantro and chilies.

Trunk Bay, St. John, U.S.V.I

A destination potluck is also great idea when you'd *like* to visit a specific country or region, but time limitations, kids or financial constraints might prevent you from doing so. Instead, go globetrotting without leaving your kitchen: invite some friends and enjoy a delicious meal, lively conversation and a great atmosphere. Here's how to do it.

Invitations: Begin at the Beginning

Invitations to your party can be as simple as a phone call, especially if it's for a small group of close friends or family. But if you want to set the scene ahead of time, a well-crafted invitation will do the job nicely. Take some plain index cards and create "postcards" from your destination, using clip art images, magazine clippings, line drawings or spare photographs. If it is to be a potluck, let each person know what type of dish to bring.

Setting the Scene

This is where you can really let those creative juices flow. Imagine your diners' experience. What do you want them to see, hear, and smell when they walk in the door? How can all these elements contribute to your overall theme? You don't have to break the bank transforming your home into another country: use things you already have at home, and check out your local dollar stores and used-goods stores for little treasures that will make a big impact. Check out your local library for sources of inspiration, and as a resource for music to enhance your setting.

Indeed, music is an important element of any global potluck. Decide what kind of "vibe" your party will have. Is it an upbeat, raucous block party, or an intimate gathering of a few friends? The type – and volume – of music can enhance this setting. Check out the world music section of your music store or library, or visit music download sites to burn a custom CD for the evening. If you purchase a CD for the party, consider using it as a door prize of sorts, at the end of the evening, for the winner of that spontaneous game of dominoes – or Twister, depending on the number of mojitos you've been serving.

Sparkling Conversation

Of course, a dinner party isn't just about the food: it's also about those hearty belly laughs and the deep connections that come along with great conversation. You can encourage interactions among your guests by providing small pieces of entertainment that support your theme. Trivia cards with questions relating to travel or food can be purchased (Travel Buff, Foodie Fight, etc.) or you can make on your own with a little research. Toss the cards around the table as part of the table setting, or set up a box near the bar or kitchen. Another way to provide entertainment is to have your guests participate in the preparations. Here are some possibilities:

- For appetizers, serve lettuce wraps that guests fill themselves
- Serve food that requires "work" such as crab claws or crawfish
- Provide a little friendly competition by having guests divide into two teams to prepare dueling desserts or dueling dishes, and offer prizes for the winning team and consolation prizes for the others

Food

This is where you don't need to be shy about asking for help. Your guests will be happy to chip in and show off their own culinary prowess, and it contributes to the communal sense of sharing food together. Generally speaking, as the host you should be responsible for the main course, but anything else is fair game.

In the next section you will find many cuisines of the world, by continent, with recipes and/or menu suggestions and interesting facts about the development of each cuisine. Every culinary tradition is so rich in history and variety, entire books could be written about each one. Lacking the time or space to do so, I have attempted to distill the essential nature of each cuisine into some basic suggestions. It is by no means an exhaustive list of countries or recipes – perhaps we'll save that for the next volume. Bon appétit – and laissez les bons temps ruler!

AFRICA

Ethiopa

It is rather fitting that we begin this journey with Ethiopia. It is sometimes re-ferred to as the cradle of civilization: some might say that's because homo sapiens may have begun here, and others (like my husband) might say it's because coffee was discovered here. After its development in the 9th century, coffee moved from Ethiopia to Egypt and Yemen, where it was converted to a stimulant. The rest, as they say, is history.

Ethiopian cuisine is rich in spices and complex layers of flavor, and it has a few major components: stews like doro wat and their accompaniment of thin, flat bread called injera, and spicy berbere paste made with fiery red chiles. Injera is difficult to make, if only because it is difficult to buy the teff flour from which it is made. If you serve a wat, or stew, to your guests, you can make the effort to make your own injera, or make do by serving pita bread, rice or couscous in its place. These Ethiopian stews, scooped up with the bread held only by the right hand, are usually made with lamb or chicken: since much of Ethiopia is either Muslim, Jewish or Eastern Orthodox Christian, pork is a non-starter for wat.

DORO WAT (CHICKEN STEW IN RED PEPPER SAUCE)

Doro Wat usually has two ingredients that I have elected to pass on here, in the interest of labor and time savings: the first is niter kebbeh, a spiced butter that, while delicious, adds a huge amount of fat (one recipe I found called for 2 cups of it – ooh, I think my arteries hardened just by writing that!). The second is berbere paste, which you can make on your own or purchase. I find that the same ingredients present in berbere are also present in the North African spice mix ras el hanout (see recipe in Northen Africa section), so I usually substitute that instead, since I usually have some on hand – the one drawback is that by using ras al hanout, you will not get that vibrant red color. It's up to you.

> 3-4 pounds bone-in chicken thighs and drumsticks
> 1/2 cup lemon juice
> 2 teaspoons salt
> 3 red onions, chopped
> 1/4 cup olive oil
> 4 cloves garlic, minced
> 1 Tablespoon minced fresh ginger
> 2 Tablespoons berbere paste or 1/2 teaspoon ground red pepper and 1 Tablespoon paprika or 2 Tablespoons ras el hanout and 1/4 teaspoon ground red pepper
> 2 cups chicken stock
> 6 hard-boiled eggs

Remove skins from thighs. Rub lemon juice and salt all over chicken pieces and allow to rest at room temperature for 30 minutes. Meanwhile, sauté onion in a large, dry sauté pan until all moisture is removed from the onions, being careful not to let them burn (this will take a while). Add olive oil, garlic, ginger, berbere paste or spices, and chicken stock. Bring to a boil and add chicken pieces back to pan. Reduce heat to low and simmer one hour or until chicken is done. When chicken is almost done, peel hard-boiled eggs, prick each several times with a fork and add to pan to warm through. Serve one egg to each person when dishing out. Serve with injera, pitas, jasmine rice or couscous.

Northern Africa:

Algeria, Libya, Morocco, and Tunisia (for Egypt, see the Middle East section)

The countries of North Africa are shaped as much by the Mediterranean Sea as by the continent on which they rest. Olive oil, fresh herbs, lemons and almonds are key flavorings shared by the many cultures that ring the Mediterranean, including those on the south shore. The strong Muslim presence also influences North African cuisine: since pork is not part of the Muslim diet, lamb, chicken and game play a dominant role. By far the most widely used grain is couscous, used ubiquitously in North Africa and revered by backpackers everywhere for its lightness in travel and its ability to cook thoroughly in less than five minutes.

The countries of North Africa share some flavors in common, such as tagines, a combination of sweet and savory spices, preserved lemons, and couscous. Moroccan cuisine is full of complex flavors, Algeria is a little more mild, and Tunisian cuisine is the spiciest of them all, with an abundant use of chiles.

MOROCCAN CHICKEN TAGINE

Moroccan tagines, named for the cone-shaped dish they are cooked in, are slow-cooked, braised stews that can include any combination of fish, chicken, lamb, vegetables, olives, fruit, nuts and spices. Tunisian tagines on the other hand more closely resemble a frittata. This recipe is a simple Moroccan version: if you do not have a tagine, you can easily substitute a tightly sealed Dutch oven or large saucepan. Serve on a cold winter night with hot couscous, and you'll warm right up.

2 Tablespoons olive oil
3-4 pounds bone-in chicken thighs and drumsticks
1 large or 2 medium onions, sliced
2 Tablespoon ras el hanout (see below)
3 cloves garlic, chopped
1 1-inch piece of ginger, chopped
1 1/2 cups chicken stock
1 cup dried apricots
1 cup drained, canned chickpeas
1/2 cup toasted slivered almonds
Hot couscous

Heat oil in large Dutch oven or saucepan. Brown the chicken pieces on all sides, remove from pan and set aside. In same pan, sauté onion for 4 minutes, then add garlic and ginger and sauté an additional 2 minutes. Add ras el hanout and stir together for one minute. Add in chicken stock, browned chicken pieces, apricots and enough water to just cover the chicken. Bring to a boil, then lower temperature, cover, and cook on medium-low heat 1-2 hours or until chicken is fully cooked and tender. Garnish with almonds and serve with hot couscous.

BASTILLA

Bastilla has many spellings, but we will stick with this version for convenience's sake. Bastilla is traditionally a pigeon pie, but lacking a dependable source of pigeon in North America, I have replaced the pigeon with rotisserie chicken available at the grocery store. The other key ingredients in a bastilla are spices, eggs, phyllo dough and almonds. If you don't have a batch of ras el hanout on hand and you don't have time to make any, there are Moroccan spice blends available but they won't necessarily have the same flavor.

If you haven't toasted almonds before, you can do it on an ungreased cookie sheet in your oven or toaster oven at 350°. Watch them closely because they can burn easily! When they have that nice golden color, take them out and give them a shake.

    1 cooked rotisserie chicken
    2 cups chicken stock or broth
    1 cup diced onion
    1/4 cup chopped fresh parsley
    3 cloves garlic, minced
    1 Tablespoon ras el hanout (see below)
    1/4 cup and 1 Tablespoon butter
    3 eggs, beaten
    2 Tablespoons slivered almonds, toasted and chopped
    8-10 sheets phyllo dough, thawed
    1 Tablespoon powdered sugar
    1/4 teaspoon cinnamon

Grease a 9" springform pan; set aside. Pull meat from chicken; set aside in refrigerator. Boil chicken stock, garlic, onion, parsley, ras el hanout and 1 Tablespoon of the butter until liquid has thickened and reduced by about one half. Add eggs and stir until eggs are fully cooked – the result will look somewhat like scrambled eggs. Stir in almonds and preheat oven to 350°. Melt remaining butter on stove or in microwave.

Layer four sheets of phyllo dough in pan so that bottom is completely covered and about half of each sheet is hanging over the edge. Brush each sheet with melted butter. Take another sheet, fold in half and lay on top of others. Add half the pulled chicken, then half the egg mixture. Take one sheet of phyllo, fold in half and place on top of egg mixture. Brush with melted butter. Repeat chicken-egg-phyllo dough layers one more time, and again brush with butter. Fold over the overhanging edges so they seal in the top sheet. Brush top with remaining melted butter.

Bake for 20-30 minutes or until top is golden brown. Allow pie to rest for 10 minutes, then remove sides of springform pan. Using a wire rack, flip bastilla on to rack and then flip again onto serving platter (so that the top is still on top). Dust with confectioner's sugar and sprinkle on cinnamon. Cut in wedges and serve hot.

RAS EL HANOUT

In Arabic, Ras el Hanout translates to "top of the shelf" or "top of the store" because the spice mix traditionally used the chef or shopkeeper's top quality items. Several different versions of this spice mix exist in North Africa, some with over 100 ingredients. This recipe is made for North American kitchens and provides the easiest way to assemble the key components. If you prefer, you can also use whole spices, toast them and grind them in a mortar and pestle or spice grinder to enhance the spices' flavors.

In my humble opinion, no one knows how to beautifully balance sweet and savory like North African and eastern Mediterranean cooks. This spice blend reminds me of a butcher I worked with at a grocery store in East Grand Rapids, who very cleverly cooked meat using a similar spice blend to lure customers to the back of the store, where he would pass out samples and easily pass his sales goal. With that incredible scent wafting through the store, those customers were like moths to the flame. Use this blend in any dish to evoke a North African flavor. It will make a big ol' batch, so feel free to halve it.

4 Tablespoons turmeric
3 Tablespoons ground black pepper
2 Tablespoons ground allspice
2 Tablespoons ground cumin
2 Tablespoons ground cardamom
2 Tablespoons cinnamon
2 Tablespoons ground coriander
2 Tablespoons dried thyme
2 Tablespoons sea salt
1 Tablespoon cayenne pepper
1 Tablespoon ground cloves
1 Tablespoon ground nutmeg
1/2 Tablespoon ground ginger
1/2 Tablespoon mace

Southern Africa:

Botswana, Lesotho, Mozambique, Namibia, South Africa, Swaziland, Zimbabwe

Southern Africa is diverse in language, culture, geography, history and cuisine. Moving from west to east, Namibia, South Africa and Mozambique grace the southern tip of the continent and face the shores of the Atlantic Ocean, Cape of Good Hope and the Indian Ocean, respectively. To the north the Kalahari Desert takes up a substantial portion of Botswana, the arid region that can boast, among other things, to be the origin of the watermelon. Word traveled fast regarding this lip-smacking treat, which found its way from the Kalahari, up to the Nile Valley by 3,000 BCE, then moved on to Greece, Rome, and the Middle East, then to Spain during the Moors' occupation. Through the slave trade it arrived on the eastern shores of North America, then traveled west to the Pacific coast, and then to Hawaii. Today pickled watermelon rind is popular in China (a major producer of the fruit) and the American South, particularly Virginia. But back to Africa.

While families still gather outdoors to cook and eat food from communal pots in small villages in Zimbabwe, others may dine on steak and locally produced wines in upscale restaurants in South Africa, and there are countless forms of dining in between. Generally speaking, grains (particularly corn and millet) and vegetables make up the majority of the diet, with meat reserved for special occasions. Those countries on the shorelines enjoy a diet rich in fish and seafood as well.

In addition to people of African descent, southern Africa is home to people from Europe and Asia, and these cultures have brought their own unique culinary traditions to the mix. As a result, a diner can find Portuguese influences in Mozambique, or a variety of Indian foods such as samosas and curries in South Africa.

BOBOTIE

When I was writing this cookbook, I asked our family doctor (who hails from South Africa) if I were to have just one recipe from South Africa, what would it be – his initial response was "I don't know, I just eat what my wife cooks for me!" Hmmm, that sounds familiar....but upon further pressing, he suggested bobotie. And what a good recommendation indeed, since it reflects the cultural mosaic of South Africa, combining the ingredients of both European (ground beef) and southeast Asian (spices and chutney) cuisines. If you like your dishes spicy, you can add in some minced hot chili pepper, or switch up your curry powder to a hotter variety.

    1 Tablespoon vegetable oil
    1 onion, chopped
    1 1/4 pounds lean ground beef (I use ground bison)
    1 slice of bread
    1 cup whole milk
    2 eggs

1 tablespoon mild or medium curry powder

1 teaspoon sugar

1 teaspoon salt

1 teaspoon ground ginger

1/4 teaspoon freshly ground pepper

1/4 cup seedless raisins or chopped apricots

2 tablespoons mango or Major Grey's chutney

2 bay leaves

Preheat oven to 350°. Heat oil in medium sauté pan and stir in onions. Cook over medium heat until soft, then add ground beef. Cook until just browned.

Soak bread in half the milk, squeeze out excess milk and mash with a fork, reserving milk. Pour milk back into other 1/2 cup, beat in eggs, and set aside.

Add curry, sugar, salt, ginger, pepper, raisins or apricots, and chutney to the beef mixture. Spoon the mixture into a greased baking dish, and place bay leaves on top.

Bake for 20 minutes, and take out of the oven. Remove bay leaves, then pour custard over meat and bake for another 20-25 minutes, or until custard has just set. Serve with yellow rice and extra chutney on the side.

PUMPKIN LEAVES WITH TOMATOES AND ONION

I thought this recipe might be more useful than how to fix the brightly colored worms that feed on the leaves of the Mopane tree. In season they may be bought dried, and sometimes smoked, from vendors who display them in traditional baskets. They can also be fried or boiled or put in relish with a little onion and tomato, or even peanut butter. But let me focus on the pumpkin:

One bunch of tenderest pumpkin leaves—clean thoroughly and strip fibers from the stem and back of leaves and cut into desired size
4 tomatoes cut into pieces
1 onion cut into rings
salt and red pepper
cooking oil

Boil 3/4 cup water in saucepan with salt and pepper. Add leaves and cover tightly. Simmer until leaves are cooked. Sauté onion until soft, add the tomatoes and cook for 5 minutes. Add this mixture to the pumpkin leaves and cook for another 5 minutes. Serve.

In Botswana they might very likely include 3 Tablespoons of pounded groundnuts or peanut butter.

SANDRA ANDERSON WHO WORKED WITH THE WORLD HEALTH
ORGANIZATION IN BOTSWANA
TUCSON, ARIZONA

CREAMED SPINACH FROM SOUTH AFRICA

All traditional Southern African food cultures gather and cook wild greens. According to Eduan Naude and Brian Shalkoff of Gramadoelas Africa Restaurant, "In each region of South Africa the local people know which leaves, pods, tendrils or flowers can be made into a vegetable stews. Great care is exercised in selecting and harvesting the plants so that the plant is not damaged."

4 bunches spinach
2 onions
1 cup warm milk
1 Tablespoon butter
1 Tablespoon flour
1/2 teaspoon freshly grated nutmeg

Chop spinach and onion coarsely and boil in salted water for 20 minutes. Strain and reserve liquid. Heat milk in small saucepan. Melt the butter in large pan and when it foams, sift in the flour. Stir with a wooden spoon till a smooth paste forms. Remove from heat and stir continuously. Slowly pour in the warm milk and stir until a smooth sauce is formed. Return to heat and simmer gently until sauce thickens. Add nutmeg and then a cup of the spinach stock. Add the spinach and onion mixture and a little more liquid, if necessary. Add salt and freshly ground pepper to taste.

SANDRA ANDERSON WHO WORKED WITH THE WORLD HEALTH
ORGANIZATION IN SOUTH AFRICA,
TUCSON, ARIZONA

ASIA and the MIDDLE EAST

Afghanistan

Hospitality in Afghanistan is the stuff of legend, and one of Calgary's newest restaurants, Ali Baba Kabob House, evokes this warm, friendly atmosphere. The casual restaurant, owned and run by Ehsan Aminzada and his wife Maryam Akbaree, features authentic Afghan dishes. When my young son Sam and I visited, Ehsan presented our food with a smile, and tried to talk to Sam, but the boy's mouth was already full of bread and his eyes were glued to the blender that was mixing doogh, a yogurt drink popular in Afghanistan.

Much of Afghan cuisine reveals its close proximity to both India and Iran: oft-used ingredients like ginger, turmeric, garlic and coriander are also popular in India, while other ingredients such as almonds, rosewater and phyllo dough tie Afghanistan's cuisine to that of the eastern Mediterranean. Kabobs are another example of a cooking method that spans borders.

MURGH KABOB (CHICKEN KABOBS)

2 – 2 1/2 pounds whole boneless, skinless chicken breasts, cut in 1-inch pieces
2 cups plain yogurt
Juice of 1 lemon
2 cloves garlic, minced
2 teaspoons coriander
1 teaspoon cinnamon
1 teaspoon turmeric
1/2 teaspoon black pepper
dash cayenne pepper

Mix everything together, and marinate at least one hour or overnight. Remove chicken pieces from marinade and thread onto skewers. Grill 10-12 minutes, or until chicken is done. Serve over rice or pilau.

China

In terms of global impact, and centuries of development of skill and knowledge of ingredients, it is difficult to top Chinese cuisine. China is the world's oldest existing society; 3,000 years ago they had already had recipes, nutritionists and chefs. The ancient Yangshao culture was the first to domesticate the pig, around 5,000 B.C.E., and they raised rice, barley and wheat. In the 2nd century B.C.E., Zhang Xian marked what would become the Silk Road to Persia, and from the Persians he brought back the concept of milling grains, along with garlic, sesame oil, walnuts, spinach, eggplant, pears, grapes, sugar beets and peas. New ingredients didn't just come from Persia, however. From Turkestan, China imported almonds; cardamom came from India and oranges from Indonesia.

Regional variety has given rise to eight major modern styles of cooking, known as the Eight Great Traditions (Anhui, Cantonese, Fujian, Hunan, Jiangsu, Shandong, Sichuan and Zhejiang). Beijing cuisine and Shanghai cuisine are sometimes included and as a whole they are then referred to as the Ten Great Traditions. Overall, there are over 80,000 dishes in the Chinese culinary repertoire, and in court cuisine attention to detail is paramount; indeed, the formal training course for Beijing duck *alone* is one full year. Artifice, or the element of surprise, is another cornerstone of Chinese cuisine, where skilled chefs will prepare a dish that looks like one thing, but is made of something entirely different.

Of course Chinese court cuisine, that which was reserved for emperors and those who could afford it, is completely different from what most people cooked at home. Limited arable land, and a limited supply of wood fuel meant that most people had to cook quickly. Stir-frying and steaming worked well in these conditions and both became foundations for the Chinese style of preparing food. Meals are served in bite-sized pieces, to accommodate the use of chopsticks: the presence of knives at the table is considered barbaric by some.

Today China's palate is changing. With the growth of a middle class, an increase in disposable income, and the increased presence of American fast food restaurants, more Chinese are eating meat and other fatty foods. An ongoing epidemiological study, known as The China Project and funded by the Universities of Oxford and Cornell and the government of China, is observing the correlation between disease and changes in dietary patterns to see if the increase in consumption of meat products is causing an increase in diseases such as cancer, diabetes and heart disease. For a country as large as China to move from a plant-based diet to one with increased animal protein will have significant environmental consequences as well, in terms of water and energy demands.

With my limited exposure and experience with Asian cooking, I would never attempt to recreate authentic Chinese court cuisine here: instead, I have included some recipes that, while somewhat Americanized, are still darn tasty. Enjoy!

GINGER BEEF

Ginger beef is wildly popular here in Alberta, almost to the point of being synonymous with Chinese food. Like other Chinese food served in the Americas, it is not necessarily the genuine article, although beef and ginger are common partners in Chinese cuisine. The version most commonly seen here in Alberta involves deep-frying battered strips of beef, which in my experience not only adds fat calories but also makes the meat awfully tough. Here is a stir-fry recipe that has all the flavor but none of that deep-fried heaviness.

1/4 cup beef stock
1/4 cup minced fresh ginger
2 Tablespoons hoisin sauce
2 Tablespoons soy sauce
2 Tablespoons rice wine vinegar
1 teaspoon sesame oil
1 1/4 pounds beef stir-fry strips
1 Tablespoon cornstarch
2 Tablespoons vegetable oil
1 pound green beans or asparagus, cut on a bias into 1" pieces
6 green onions, cut on a bias into 1" pieces
2 cups cooked rice

Mix beef stock, ginger, hoisin sauce, soy sauce, vinegar and oil together in a small bowl and set aside. Toss beef strips with cornstarch. Heat oil in large wok or sauté pan and add beef. Cook until just done, remove and keep warm. Toss beans or asparagus and green onions into pan, adding more oil if necessary, and sauté two minutes or until crisp-tender. Move veggies to outside of pan, and add sauce, allowing it to cook for one minute, then add beef back to pan and stir through, allowing mixture to thicken. Serve over hot rice.

GRILLED SALMON WITH EAST-WEST SPICE RUB AND ORANGE-SOY GLAZE

We had this salmon over the summer at a friend's barbeque and I had to have the recipe! The salmon takes on the flavor of the rub so beautifully, and also makes for a pretty plate. A simple basmati rice and some lemony green beans are a delicious accompaniment; maybe even a good loaf of sourdough, too. Make sure you get a lot of the sauce on the fish as it cooks. If I'm doing this for 8 I usually get a big, long piece of salmon and just toss that baby on the grill. You could also just toss some fresh asparagus on the grill at the end of the salmon and then you're not doing many dishes! This is great for summertime, but keep it in mind when entertaining all year long. Furthermore, children love this! Bon appétit!

1 Tablespoon sugar
1/2 Tablespoon five-spice powder
1/2 Tablespoon ground coriander
1/2 Tablespoon ground black pepper
1/2 teaspoon salt
3 – 3 x 1/2" orange rind strips
1/2 cup fresh orange juice
1/2 cup low sodium soy sauce
1/3 cup honey
2 Tablespoons minced green onion
1 Tablespoon minced fresh ginger
1/2 Tablespoon sesame oil
4 garlic cloves, minced
1 3-inch stick cinnamon
8 6-ounce salmon fillets
cooking spray

1/4 cup thinly sliced green onion
1 Tablespoon toasted sesame seeds

To prepare spice mixture, combine first 5 ingredients in a small bowl. To prepare glaze, combine orange rind and next 8 ingredients (through cinnamon) in a saucepan. Bring to a boil. Reduce heat, and simmer 10 minutes. Strain through a sieve; discard solids.

Rub the fillets with spice mixture. Cover; refrigerate 30 minutes. Place skin sides down on a grill rack coated with cooking spray. Grill 16 minutes, covered, or until fish flakes easily when tested with a fork, basting occasionally with glaze. Remove skin, discard. Arrange fillets on a platter; sprinkle with sliced onions and sesame seeds.

LISA MALONEY, BOULDER, COLORADO

MONKEY (KING) BREAD

I must start with a caveat: other than the inspiration for this recipe, Monkey King Bread has *nothing whatsoever to do with authentic Chinese cuisine*. But trust me, keep reading!

Ever since visiting an exhibition on the Chinese tale of the Monkey King at the Grand Rapids Children's Museum, my kids have been fascinated with stories about him. In one story, Monkey King steals enchanted peaches from the Jade Emperor's peach orchard, then swipes some magic buns from the bakers in the Emperor's palace. Both treats give him special powers that he uses to get into quite a bit of mischief, until the Buddha puts him in his place. I've combined this story with traditional American "monkey bread" to create a sweet treat that's great for breakfast or snack time. Serve this to your kids and enjoy while you indulge them in a story of the Monkey King! Those with older kids could also watch *The Forbidden Kingdom*, a film with Jackie Chan and Jet Li that came out in 2008 and features Monkey King in the story line. By the way, India has its own version of Monkey King and some historians believe the legend actually traveled from India to China.

Be careful not to let the dinner roll dough set out too long after thawing, or it can over-proof quickly, especially in warm summer months.

- 24 ounces frozen dinner roll dough, just thawed
- 3/4 cup packed brown sugar
- 2/3 cup instant vanilla pudding mix
- 1/4 cup white sugar
- 2 teaspoons ground cinnamon
- 1/2 teaspoon ground ginger
- 1 cup drained diced canned peaches
- 1/2 cup chopped pecans
- 1/2 cup (1 stick) butter

Preheat oven to 350° and grease and flour a 9 or 10 inch tube pan. Melt butter and put in small bowl. Mix sugars, pudding mix, cinnamon and ginger together in a shallow bowl or pie pan. Cut each roll in half (I just use kitchen shears), dip in butter then roll around in sugar mixture. Place each sugared roll in tube pan until one layer is complete. Sprinkle on diced peaches and 1/2 of pecans. Repeat roll procedure until second layer is complete. Take any remaining butter, add remaining pecans and enough sugar mixture to create a crumbly streusel topping and sprinkle on top of second layer. Bake 35-40 minutes or until top layer is a deep golden brown. Let stand a few minutes and turn pan over onto serving platter.

Serve immediately or up to one hour after baking.

TEA EGGS

These are often served on Chinese New Year, but they are fun to make any time. Simmering the eggs in tea creates a wonderful marbled effect on the eggs that makes them look like works of art, and adds a subtle salty-sweetness. Be careful when tapping the eggs!

    6 eggs
    2 Tablespoons loose black tea leaves (you can open up tea bags too)
    2 Tablespoons soy sauce
    1 teaspoon salt
    1 1/2 teaspoons Chinese five-spice powder

Place the eggs in a saucepan and cover with water. Bring to a gentle boil, reduce heat and simmer for five minutes. Remove from heat, drain and cover with cold water. When the eggs have cooled enough to hold by hand, very gently tap each one with the back of a spoon, creating cracks all over the egg. Drain the pan, put the eggs back in and cover with fresh water. Add remaining ingredients to the water and gently stir through.

Put the pan back on the stove, bring to a boil again, reduce heat and cover. Simmer gently for 40 minutes, stirring occasionally. After 40 minutes, remove pan from the burner and allow the pan to sit for one hour.

Peel the eggs and serve immediately, or refrigerate and eat within two days.

WALKING BEGGARS' CHICKEN

This is based on the traditional Chinese recipe for Beggars' Chicken, a dish whose name belies the artful process of putting it together. It comes with a story: one day a beggar, desperate for food, stole a chicken from a local farmer and began to cook it over a fire. Hearing the sound of an approaching horseman, the beggar quickly wrapped the bird in some lotus leaves and buried it in the ground near the fire. The horseman, who turned out to be the aggrieved farmer, saw no stolen chicken and continued on his way. When the coast was clear, the beggar unearthed his chicken, now cooked in hard clay, to discover it had been perfectly steamed in the aroma of the lotus leaves.

Depending on the story you read, sometimes the farmer is replaced by the tax man, or others, but the essence of the story remains the same. A beggar hastily buries a chicken in clay and it is magically cooked to perfection. The modern preparation of Beggars' Chicken is very complicated and time-consuming: patrons usually need to order it ahead of time, and it is often reserved for preferred guests at restaurants. It involves wrapping a whole, marinated chicken tightly with lotus leaves, then encasing that in either clay or salt dough, so that it is sealed shut. It is then roasted on low heat over several hours.

Most North American cooks will be hard pressed to find lotus leaves, not to mention the right type of mud preferred by Chinese chefs. I have taken the essence of several recipes and converted it into something that can be easily made, and eaten by hand. These can be served as appetizers, or two can be served as a main course.

2 chicken breast halves, each cut in four equal pieces
2 Tablespoons soy sauce
1 Tablespoon rice wine vinegar
1 Tablespoon minced fresh ginger
1/4 pound ground pork
1/4 cup finely chopped green onions

2 Tablespoons finely chopped celery
2 Tablespoons finely chopped oyster or shitake mushrooms
1 Tablespoon sesame oil
1 Tablespoon soy sauce
2 teaspoons hoisin sauce
8 frozen dinner rolls, thawed and covered with damp towel
flour
egg wash (1 egg, beaten, mixed with 1/4 cup water)

Combine 2 Tablespoons of soy sauce, rice wine vinegar and ginger to make marinade, and pour over chicken pieces to marinate for one hour.

In small sauté pan, brown ground pork; when almost cooked through, add green onions, celery and mushrooms. Continue cooking until vegetables are soft. Add sesame oil, 1 Tablespoon of soy sauce and hoisin sauce and stir through. Set aside.

Grease a baking sheet and preheat oven to 375°. Roll out one dinner roll to about 5" in diameter on floured surface. Place one chicken piece near the middle, and top with pork mixture. Fold dough over, seal edges and brush top with egg wash. Place on baking sheet, and repeat for remaining seven pieces.

Bake for 25-35 minutes, or until dough is golden brown and a thermometer inserted into the middle reads 165°. Serve hot.

India

India, perhaps more than any other country, stands as the ultimate example of how food has traveled the globe, with one culture's cuisine influencing another. The complex cuisine of India is an amalgamation of many different cultures, and conversely its food has spread across the globe along with its people as they traveled to the Americas, the Caribbean, and South Africa in particular.

India's culinary heritage springs mainly from its neighbors, and from those who traveled from the Middle East: China brought rice, Indonesia brought spices, particularly to southern India, and the Moghuls brought the concept of baking in a clay oven, or tandoor. Near the end of the 12th century, Moghul invaders came from central Asia and established rule that lasted, in some form, for over four hundred years: in Northern India, where the Moghul influence was strongest, meat kebabs, sweets, nuts, and cooking in tandoor ovens is more common, reflecting the Persian influence.

In an attempt to get around the overland trade route to India, Vasco de Gama sailed to Calcutta in 1498, and in the 1500s – 1600's, governments from England,

France, Denmark and Portugal began setting up trading posts and buying land, and competed in their attempts to colonize the region. The last Moghul Emperor's reign ended in 1605, five years after the English had established the East India Trading Company. The English had already begun trade agreements with the Emperor, and after the end of his rule the East India Company's influence became stronger and stronger until India became an English colony.

England's legacy on Indian cuisine is somewhat limited: mulligatawny (from the Tamil *milagu-tunir*, or pepper-water) and the curious name of "curry" can be attributed to English rule: some believe the word curry, which didn't originally appear in Indian culture, to be a mispronunciation of the *kari* leaf. Other English contributions were Major Grey's chutney, and Worcestershire sauce, of all things. Portugal also left their mark with vindaloo, popular in Goa, which comes from the Portuguese *vindalho* (*vinho* for vinegar and *aldos* for garlic). Portugal also introduced cashews, pineapples, tomatoes, potatoes and chilies to the Indian diet. Indeed, prior to the discovery of New World chilies, Indian food was not as spicy as it is today.

Later, when slavery was abolished in the English-held colonies of the Caribbean, plantation owners had to quickly replace their labor force. As a result, Indian laborers arrived as indentured servants. They were still forced to work the land, but at the end of the payment of their passage they were free. These "East Indians" brought their culinary traditions with them, and as a result you can still find curries and roti a common sight in these islands, particularly in Trinidad where Indian populations were strongest.

My husband and I eat Indian food about once a week, ever since I read there may be a connection between turmeric and low rates of Alzheimer's disease. That is one of many, many health benefits associated with Indian cuisine, primarily because of the ginger, garlic and capsaicin (the "active ingredient" in chiles), all of which we are learning new things about in terms of their abilities to prevent and fight disease. Yummy food you can feel good about – I love it!

CHILI CHICKEN

This is an easy dish to make so we have it fairly frequently. In most Indian households, spice measurements and ratios are not precise. You just throw a little of this and a lot of that, completely based on your preference. If you don't have an ingredient, you can omit it completely, and add a bit extra of something else. So feel free to play around with the quantities. If you deep-fry the chicken pieces instead of sautéing them, the dish can be called Chicken 65 which is quite a popular offering on the streets of Mumbai, India.

1 pound boneless, skinless chicken thighs
Marinade:
1 teaspoon cayenne pepper
1 teaspoon chili powder
1 teaspoon turmeric
1 teaspoon ground cumin
1 teaspoon ground coriander
1 1/2 Tablespoons soy sauce
1 Tablespoon fresh ginger, mashed to a pulp
1 Tablespoon fresh garlic, mashed to a pulp
1 Tablespoon spicy chili sauce
1 1/2 Tablespoons rice vinegar
salt to taste
1 medium to large onion, sliced lengthwise
1 small green pepper (capsicum), sliced into thin strips
2 Tablespoons oil
2 Tablespoons finely chopped cilantro leaves

Cut chicken thighs into bite sized pieces. Marinate for at least four hours, preferably overnight. Cut onion and green pepper. Heat oil. Sauté onion and green pepper until onion is soft, but not mushy. Remove onion and green pepper from pan. Add chicken and sauté until chicken is browned. Cover pan and cook chicken. At the last stages add the sautéed onions and green pepper to the chicken and let all the flavors blend together. The dish should be saucy, but not runny. Garnish with cilantro leaves and serve with hot rice.

VINITA DOWD, CALGARY, ALBERTA

BEEF KABABS

I usually make these when entertaining as they are so easy, and so tasty with drinks and chips. In our household, it is also eaten stuffed into rotis, pitas, or hot dog buns.

 1 pound lean or extra lean ground beef
 2 teaspoons cayenne
 2 teaspoons chili powder
 1 teaspoon turmeric
 2 teaspoons ground cumin
 1 teaspoon ground coriander
 1 Tablespoon crushed fresh ginger
 1 Tablespoon crushed fresh garlic
 3 Tablespoons finely chopped cilantro
 1 Tablespoon oil
 Juice of 1/2 lime or lemon
 1/4 onion, finely chopped (optional)
 salt to taste

Mix all ingredients together. Shape into rolls approximately 3 inches long, and 1/2 inch wide. Do not flatten. Grill on barbeque or in oven. Serve hot. Usually these are eaten as appetizers.

VINITA DOWD, CALGARY, ALBERTA

VEGETABLE PULAV

This is just a basic pulav. There are many versions. You can change things up by adding a bit of coconut milk for a coconutty flavour. You can also add crisply fried onions and cashews to it at the end stages as a garnish.

1 cup basmati rice (washed 3-4 times and drained)
1 onion, finely sliced lengthwise
4 pods cardamom
4 whole cloves
1 cinnamon stick
2 bay leaves
1/2 cup frozen mixed vegetables
2 chicken bouillon cubes (optional)
2 cups water
3 Tablespoons oil
salt to taste

Heat oil in large sauté pan. Add cardamom, cloves, cinnamon stick, and bay leaves. Do not let oil smoke. After a minute or two, add onion. Sauté until onion is light brown. Add washed rice. Sauté rice for a couple of minutes. Add water. Add salt and bouillon cubes and bring to a boil. Add frozen veggies, and cover and cook until water has evaporated.

VINITA DOWD, CALGARY, ALBERTA

The Middle East:

Egypt, Iran, Iraq, Jordan, Lebanon, and Syria

The term "Middle East" was coined when those doing the coining still believed Europe was the center of the earth and everything else was relative. Hence, China was "far east" and those countries situated at the eastern shore of the Mediterranean were the "middle east." While the term may no longer be timely, it is a name that is immediately recognizable for most.

Although today we think of the Middle East as a dry, desert climate, it was at one time a fertile region that gave rise to major civilizations and culinary foundations. The earliest known fossils date to about 10,000 B.C.E., and provide evidence of hunting, and growing wheat, barley, lentils and peas; moreover, the Sumerians created one of the world's first written language systems.

In addition, many foods and dishes we may consider native to other cultures arose here: wheat and beer are native to the area; coffee was converted from a bean to a stimulant, and bread was originally baked here, along with the method for harvesting and milling grains. Not a bad start.

Tapas, which we associate with Spanish cuisine, are simply an adaptation from *mezze*, a Middle Eastern style of creating several small dishes that was imported into Spain during the Moors' occupation – along with orange and almond groves. Indeed, the culinary legacy of traders and conquerors from the eastern Mediterranean is worldwide. China may have invented noodles, but it was traders from the Middle East who showed them how to mill grains.

It is an incredibly diverse region, home to multitudes of religions and ethnicities. To do each one service would be another book entirely – so in the meantime, enjoy these versions of traditional Middle Eastern dishes.

CHICKEN SHAWARMA

To make truly authentic shawarma, one would need a giant upright spit from which to carve slices of meat (think Turkish döner or Greek gyros). Barring that, the best way to replicate the flavor is to grill or broil well-marinated cuts of meat. Shawarmas are found throughout the Arab world, with several variations, but they are popular worldwide, probably because of a) the great flavor and b) like tacos and sandwiches, they can be eaten on the go. Fresh mint and parsley aren't usually added to the finished product, but I like the freshness it adds.

   1 cup plain yogurt
   1 1/2 Tablespoons lemon juice
   1 Tablespoon minced garlic
   1 teaspoon allspice
   1/4 teaspoon salt
   1/4 teaspoon ground black pepper
   1/4 teaspoon ground cayenne pepper
   1 1/4 pounds chicken breast

Pita Bread
1 Tablespoon chopped fresh mint
1 Tablespoon chopped fresh parsley
Lettuce leaves
Tomato Slices
Tahini sauce, tzaziki or hummus

Combine yogurt, lemon juice, garlic, allspice, salt, pepper and cayenne pepper in small bowl. Slice chicken breast into thin slices and add to yogurt sauce – marinate for at least 6 hours or overnight.

Grill chicken pieces on a wire rack on grill until done. Serve in pitas with lettuce, tomato and choice of sauce or spread.

HUMMUS

Lionel is chief hummus maker at our house, and this recipe is consistently delicious. We like to have it with a big platter of raw veggies, crackers, torn up pita bread, you name it. It also makes a delicious sandwich spread for a veggie sandwich.

1 can garbanzo beans (chickpeas)
3 Tablespoons tahini, or more to taste
salt and pepper to taste
1/2 Tablespoon cumin
1 teaspoon sweet paprika
1 teaspoon fennel seeds (optional)
1/2 head roasted garlic
2 teaspoons lemon juice
olive oil

Drain the beans, reserving the liquid. In a food processor, combine all ingredients with 2/3 of the reserved liquid. If your hummus is too thick, continue to add more liquid a bit at a time. Place hummus in a bowl, give a generous drizzle of olive oil, and a splash of paprika for color and taste. Serve with.... anything you want!

CINDY LOZA, MARION, IOWA

MIDDLE EASTERN SEVEN-LAYER DIP

Many people are familiar with seven-layer dip, which usually features Tex-Mex ingredients like refried beans, salsa, sour cream and cheese. This is similar, but features fresh-tasting ingredients found in eastern Mediterranean cooking. It goes really well with warmed pita bread torn in pieces, but crackers will do just fine.

2 cups hummus
1 cup chopped baby spinach
1 cup roasted red pepper tapenade
1/2 cup drained chickpeas
1/4 cup chopped fresh parsley
1 tablespoon chopped fresh mint
1/2 cup crumbled feta or plain goat cheese
1/4 cup chopped green onions or cucumber
1/4 cup chopped black olives

Spread hummus on a large plate or shallow serving dish. Sprinkle baby spinach on top, and spoon tapenade, then chickpeas, on top of spinach. Toss parsley and mint together, and sprinkle on top of chickpeas. Sprinkle remaining ingredients in the order given.

Nepal

In more ways than one, Nepal's geography has dictated its cuisine. First, for centuries, the landlocked nation's mountains isolated it from outside influence, allowing a unique cuisine to develop. Secondly, within a relatively small amount of land (approximately 550 miles by 125 miles), Nepal has three vastly different ecosystems, each producing unique foods and cuisines: the high Himalayan region, the Tarai lowlands, and the mountains themselves. Indeed, Nepal boasts the largest elevation change of any country, from the lowlands to the top of Mount Everest (29,029 feet).

Although traditional foods are still made in most homes, Nepal's cuisine also now reflects its exposure to the west through tourists and mountain climbers, and its proximity to India, China and Tibet has allowed for the incorporation of ingredients such as curries, and pickled radish. Generally speaking diners in Nepal eat two main meals per day, one mid-morning and one in the evening, with snacks in between. Meals do not usually begin with appetizers, but if you want to serve some, traditional snacks such as spiced nuts, samosas and vegetable fritters would do nicely. Roti, a flatbread, could also be served with chutney.

Diners still commonly eat with the fingers of their right hand, using rice to scoop saucy dishes of vegetables, lentils and/or meats, a custom that is shared by other countries such as India and Morocco. Water is provided before and after eating to wash one's hands, and silverware is often used as well as a result of western influence.

Although there are regional variations within the national cuisine, as a rule Nepali cuisine features fresh ingredients, inventive uses of spices and aromatics, liberal use of rice and other grains, vegetables, and a limited use of meat, usually saved for special days. Rice in particular is featured at every meal and snack, either boiled, fried, blended into sweets, or used in flour or pressed rice flakes. It is central to Nepali cuisine and culture, used not only as food but also as offerings in sacred and communal ceremonies, and in birth, marriage and death rituals.

DAAL BHAT (LENTILS AND RICE)

This is the delicious national dish of Nepal, often served with some spicy atchar or chutney on the side, which makes it always different and interesting. If I had to eat one dish the rest of my life, it would be Daal Bhat. Many Nepalis still eat it every morning about 9-10 am and again at the end of the day.

    1 cup lentils (yellow, orange, red, green or black)- soak for an hour.
    1/2 teaspoon salt
    1/2 teaspoon turmeric powder
    2 Tablespoons clarified butter (ghee) or melted butter
    1 onion chopped
    2 cloves of garlic finely chopped
    2.5 cm piece of ginger finely chopped
    1/2 teaspoon cumin seeds
    1/4 teaspoon ground coriander
    1/4 cup chopped fresh coriander (cilantro) leaves

Soak lentils for one hour, drain, then boil in 1 1/2 cups water with salt and turmeric until tender and lentils have thoroughly absorbed the water. Sauté onion, garlic and ginger in butter till golden. Add cumin seeds and coriander powder and sauté a few seconds, and add to lentils. Cover. Serve hot on rice, garnished with chopped coriander leaves. Serves 4-5 persons.

SANDRA ANDERSON WHO WORKED WITH THE WORLD HEALTH
ORGANIZATION IN NEPAL, 1986-89
TUCSON, ARIZONA

Thailand

Thai cuisine has caught on quickly in North America, and with good reason: the food is, overall, very healthy, flavorful, quick to prepare, and for gustatory daredevils, offers plenty of heat in its chili-based dishes.

Thailand has a lot to be proud of, as a country and as a contributor to world cuisine. It is the world's leading producer of rice; it enjoys a treasure-trove of fresh and saltwater fish and seafood from its shores and inland waterways; and it was recently named as one of the world's foremost cuisines, after France, Italy and Hong Kong.

Much of Thai cuisine includes basic flavors of lemongrass, Thai basil (holy basil), garlic, galangal (related to ginger), pepper, fish sauce or nam pla, and curry. Thai food is also known for its fiery hot chilies, although these were unknown to Thai cooks prior to their introduction by Portuguese traders in the 16th century. One of the hottest dishes is prik khee noo, made with sauce so hot it will make a tiger cry (this is a new adaptation of the title, which used to refer to the toughness of the meat). Basic dishes include salads or *yum*, soups, *kaeng* (any dish that is soupy or curry-like), and rice and noodle dishes such as the familiar pad thai.

Although Thailand has a prominent Buddhist culture, it is not strictly vegetarian: beef, pork, chicken, fish and seafood are mainstays of Thai culture, all coming in a distant second to the ubiquitous rice. The average Thai consumes 3/4 of a pound of uncooked rice per day: compare that to the average American, eating 1/2 of a pound of rice per month and you get a sense of how important rice is to the Thai diet.

If hosting a Thai dinner party, you can serve your food in courses, even though traditionally all the food is normally brought out at the same time. For a first course, you could serve a common "finger salad" with many options for guests to sample and place in lettuce leaves. It would be a great "entrée" into the evening, providing sustenance and entertainment. Follow with a curry or two, and end with fresh fruit or a dessert of coconut rice. For an easy weeknight supper, here's an easy pad thai recipe.

PAD THAI

Tamarind paste is one of the ingredients in authentic pad thai, but it can be hard to come by. In a pinch, you can substitute ketchup (I know, I know) or hoisin sauce to give it that same sweet-sour richness. No one will know, I promise.

Once you have all your ingredients ready to go, pad thai is made very quickly so make sure you have everything you need before you start, and be ready to serve it minutes after you start cooking.

  8 ounces rice stick noodles
  1 Tablespoon white sugar
  1/4 cup soy sauce
  1/4 cup rice wine vinegar

2 Tablespoons fish sauce

1 Tablespoon sesame oil

1 Tablespoon tamarind paste

Juice of one fresh lime

dash hot chili pepper sauce

2 Tablespoons vegetable oil

1/2 pound shrimp, peeled and deveined

1 cup diced extra-firm tofu

3 cloves garlic, minced

2 eggs, lightly beaten

3 cups bean sprouts

6 green onions, chopped

1 cup chopped dry roasted peanuts

1 cup chopped fresh cilantro

1 cup chopped cucumber

2 limes, cut into wedges

Soften rice noodles according to package directions and set aside. Stir together sugar, soy sauce, rice wine vinegar, fish sauce, sesame oil, tamarind paste, lime juice and chili pepper sauce in a small bowl and set aside. Heat oil in large sauté pan on medium-high heat, and add shrimp and tofu. When shrimp is about halfway cooked, toss in minced garlic. When shrimp is just cooked, move everything to the outer rim and pour in eggs. Allow eggs to partially set without stirring, then toss in noodles, bean sprouts and green onions, stirring everything together quickly. Add sauce and stir through. Serve on plates, and toss peanuts, cilantro and cucumber on top of each serving. Garnish with lime wedges. Makes 4 servings.

Turkey

Straddling East and West, both geographically and culturally, Turkey is a unique country that balances relations with both hemispheres. Life in Turkey is deeply connected to food: it is not just sustenance, but tradition, community and reverence. This is a country that produced poets that wrote odes to food, and many of their proverbs use food as metaphor. Dishes have poetic names like "The Sultan Liked It," "Old Woman's Neck" and "The Imam Fainted." Hospitality is also taken very seriously here, as evidenced by the proverb, "A guest brings ten blessings – he takes one with him and leaves nine."

Turkey has an amazing culinary history. From the mid-15th century to the 18th century, Sultans of the Ottoman Empire built or expanded massive kitchens at Istanbul's Topkapi Palace, employing hundreds of workers, and held banquets on a huge scale (much of their material wealth came from control of the lucrative overland spice route, connecting Europe and Asia). For one wedding feast alone, the festivities lasted three weeks and the menu called for 50,000 chickens, among other things. The kitchen staff could serve as many as 10,000 people per day and double that on special occasions.

Kitchens of Topkapi Palace.

While your own dinner party might not be quite so extravagant, you can still wow your guests by creating a dining environment that evokes the traditional Turkish banquet. Spread pillows on the floor, and place food in platters on a low table in the center of the room. Food is traditionally eaten communally, with people scooping food from a common platter with either a fork, or piece of bread, or both.

Turks love their sweets: homemade versions of traditional desserts are often exchanged as gifts. Baklava is an art form here, and halva is a traditional sweet that is served in many forms. A version of halva made with flour is traditionally served after a person has died, and again 40 days later. And anyone familiar with C.S. Lewis' story of *The Lion, The Witch and the Wardrobe* will know just how far a boy will go for a piece of Turkish Delight, or lokum, the sweetened confection that comes in many flavors and colors.

Many dishes, such as meze and pilav, reflect Turkey's connection to the Middle East. Meze is a group of small dishes, usually accompanied by beverages, and served at a gathering of friends. The concept is Persian in origin, and came to Turkey under rather curious circumstance. Sultan Süleyman the Magnificent conquered the Persian Safavids in 1538, and brought back the idea of royal tasters with him (these were the unlucky fellows who tasted the Sultan's food first, to make sure it wasn't poisonous). The taster's dishes were called *meze*, the Persian word for pleasant taste. The concept caught on among privileged society, and the rest is history.

Other dishes reveal Turkey's long history of trade with other countries, such as China, which shared with Turkey the concept of the stuffed noodle, or dumpling: in Turkey, this is eaten today as *manti* – in China, it is the wonton. To hold a Turkish-themed potluck, you could present food as a series of small meze dishes, including small kebabs, or instead, host a formal Turkish dinner. Be sure to provide some Turkish music in the background to transport your guests.

Oh, and by the way, for those who always wondered if there was a connection, the reason turkeys are called turkey, is because it was the Turks who originally introduced the bird to European diners, thus the name turkey for our Thanksgiving bird. In Turkey, it is called hindi, or Indian, referring to the misnamed "Indians" of North America.

IMAM BAYILDI (THE IMAM FAINTED)

This dish comes with a tale about a Turkish Imam (Muslim leader) who married the daughter of a wealthy olive oil merchant. The Imam, being quite the gourmand, was delighted with his bride's dowry of twelve jars of olive oil. For the first twelve days of their marriage, the wife prepared a special dish of eggplant in olive oil, which became his favorite. When day thirteen arrived, there was no eggplant at the meal. When asked, the bride informed her husband that they had gone through all the olive oil and would now have to buy some more. Shocked by the answer, the Imam fainted. Since that day, according to the legend, the dish has been known as Imam Bayildi (another version has the Imam fainting because it's just that good). It is usually served at room temperature or cold, with pita bread to help scoop out the eggplant.

  1 large eggplant
  2 teaspoons salt
  1 cup diced onion
  4 cloves garlic, minced
  2 fresh tomatoes, diced
  1 teaspoon sugar
  1/2 cup fresh parsley
  1/4 cup olive oil

Cut off the stem of the eggplant and slice lengthwise. If desired, slice off a small, very shallow section of each peel side so that eggplant halves will lay flat. On cut side, make several slits in the eggplant, being careful not to go all the way through. Sprinkle salt generously on the cut side of both halves and place them cut side down in a colander for one hour. Rinse thoroughly with water to remove salt and pat dry.

Heat olive oil in large sauté pan and cook eggplant cut-side down for about five minutes, or until browned. Remove with tongs and place in shallow baking dish.

Sauté onion, garlic, tomatoes, sugar and parsley in remaining olive oil until vegetables are softened. Season to taste with salt and pepper. Divide mixture evenly and place on eggplant halves. Preheat oven to 350° and bake for 30 minutes. Remove from oven and allow them to cool to room temperature. Can also be made ahead of time and served cold.

Imam Biyaldi, before baking.

THE SULTAN LIKED IT, OR HÜNKAR BEGENDI

This is a traditional recipe of Turkey, and it's easy to see why it's popular. Meat, garlic and onion, warm cheese sauce - it's sophisticated comfort food. You can also grill the eggplant in this dish, which will give it a nice smoky edge.

The eggplant is a nutritional powerhouse: it has antiviral and antioxidant properties, and is full of bioflavonoids that may help prevent disease. Guess that kind of makes up for the meat, butter, whole milk and cheese....

2 Tablespoons olive oil
1 1/2 pounds boneless lamb, beef, bison or chicken, cut into 1 inch cubes
1 onion, sliced
2 fresh tomatoes, seeded and diced
2 garlic cloves, chopped
1 Tablespoon tomato paste
1 large eggplant
2 Tablespoons lemon juice (for color)
2 teaspoons salt
3 Tablespoons butter
3 Tablespoons flour
1/2 cup whole milk, room temperature
1/4 cup shredded mozzarella cheese
salt and pepper to taste

Preheat oven to 450°. Prick eggplant with sharp knife then place on shallow baking pan and roast for 30-40 minutes, or until softened. Allow to cool somewhat, then slice off the tops and peel. Pour water into a large bowl, and add lemon juice and salt. Scoop out large chunks of pulp from eggplants and soak them in the bowl for about 10-15 minutes. Remove from bowl, and remove as much water as possible. Mash the pulp and set aside.

Heat oil in a large sauté pan. Add meat and cook until just done. Remove and set aside. In same pan, adding more oil if necessary, sauté onion and garlic for 2 minutes. Return meat to pan and add tomatoes, tomato paste, stirring everything together. Cover and cook on low heat for about 15 minutes, adding water or stock if sauce dries out.

Meanwhile, melt butter in saucepan and add flour to make a roux. Stir until blended, then add eggplant pulp, making sure there are no large chunks. Slowly pour in the milk and beat with a whisk. Add cheese and stir until blended. Add salt and pepper to taste. Serve as sauce or accompaniment to meat.

BAKLAVA

This delightful little dessert is shared by many cuisines of the former Ottoman Empire, but it is very well known in Turkey and comes in several forms. Baklava was served to the Sultan and his guests at the Topkapi Palace, and was part of a ceremonial procession during Ramadan known as Baklava Alayi. It is usually made with pistachios or walnuts, although you can use whatever nuts you have on hand.

1 pound walnuts, finely chopped
1 teaspoon ground cinnamon
1/4 teaspoon ground cloves
1 Tablespoon brown sugar
1 16-ounce package phyllo dough, thawed
1 cup butter, melted
1 cup sugar
1 cup water
1/2 cup honey
1 teaspoon vanilla extract
1 Tablespoon grated lemon zest

Preheat oven to 350°. Butter a 9 x 13 baking dish. Toss nuts, brown sugar, cloves and cinnamon together. Remove phyllo from packaging, cut it in half to fit the dish, and place stack on a lightly damp cloth, then cover with another damp cloth.

Place 6 sheets of phyllo in the bottom of baking pan. Brush generously with butter. Sprinkle about 1/4 cup of filling on top. Add two layers of phyllo dough on top, brush with butter, then add two more layers of dough. Sprinkle on nut mixture again, and continue these layers until all ingredients are used, using six sheets of phyllo dough for top layer. Using a sharp knife or pizza cutter, cut baklava about 1/2 inch deep in four strips lengthwise, then diagonally to form diamond shapes. Bake 40-50 minutes, or until golden.

Meanwhile, heat sugar and water to a boil in a small saucepan. Add honey, vanilla and lemon zest, reduce heat and simmer for 20 minutes.

When baklava has finished baking, remove it from the oven and immediately drizzle the syrup over it. Allow to cool completely before serving.

NOAH'S PUDDING (ASHURE)

The story of Noah is a great one for remembering that Christians, Muslims and Jews share a common heritage, since he is mentioned in the Bible, the Qur'an and the Torah. This dish is often served at "interfaith dialogue" meetings, and in Muslim countries in particular it is made in large batches and shared with neighbors and with those less fortunate. Indeed, it is a great dish for serving crowds in warmer climates, because it is served cold, it's delicious, and even though it's a dessert it is nutritionally complete: the beans provide protein, the grains provide complex carbohydrates, and the fruit provides vitamins.

In the Muslim tradition, Noah finally reaches land and he and the rest of the family scrounge around for what little food is left. They throw everything together, and the result is ashure, or Noah's Pudding: a Mesopotamian version of "Stone Soup," if you will. Thousands of years ago Noah's family shared what they had with each other, and today the tradition continues.

Traditionally ashure is made with wheat, but you can play around with any combination of grains, nuts and dried fruits – rice, barley (used here), oats, any would work, but you may need to alter your cooking times accordingly. Generally speaking, use enough water to cook the grain completely, then add more water and everything else, saving the nuts for garnish.

1/2 cup barley
1/2 cup drained and rinsed white kidney beans
1/2 cup drained and rinsed chickpeas
1/4 cup sugar
3/4 teaspoon vanilla
1/4 teaspoon cinnamon
5 apricots, soaked in water overnight
5 dried figs, cut in pieces
1/2 cup raisins
2 Tablespoons toasted pine nuts

Rinse the barley in a sieve to remove starch. Pour it and 1 1/2 cups of water in a medium saucepan and bring to a boil. Reduce heat to low, cover and simmer about 25 minutes or until barley is cooked. Add another 2 1/2 cups of water, and all remaining ingredients *except* pine nuts. Bring to a boil, reduce heat to medium-low, and simmer for about 40 minutes or until mixture is thick and syrupy. Allow mixture to cool in the refrigerator and serve cold in six individual bowls, with one teaspoon of pine nuts on top of each as garnish.

AUSTRALIA and the SOUTH PACIFIC

Australia

Luarna Duncan taught at my son Elliott's school in Calgary, Alberta, as part of a teacher exchange. Now back in the land down under, she volunteered these treasured family recipes for the cookbook. Some are very popular in Australia, with many versions floating around, but these are the tried and true interpretations of Luarna's family, handed down through the generations.

FAIRY BREAD

A must at any child's birthday party.

> Fresh sliced white bread
> Butter or margarine, softened
> Candy sprinkles

Simply butter the bread and cover with sprinkles. Cut off the crusts and enjoy.

LUARNA DUNCAN, WODONGA, AUSTRALIA

LAMINGTONS

Lamingtons are served for morning or afternoon tea, and are sold at all Australian bakeries. Read the children's book *Possum Magic* by Mem Fox to see more of this Aussie delight.

They can be kept a couple of days without the cream filling. A basic plain cake (packet cake mix) can be used for this recipe.

    8 ounces self-rising flour
    6 ounces sugar
    4 ounces butter
    3 eggs
    1/2 cup milk (may vary)
    pinch of salt
    one drop vanilla extract

Sift flour and salt together; set aside. Cream butter and sugar, and beat in eggs one at a time. Add vanilla. Slowly add sifted dry ingredients alternatively with milk to form a light batter. Simply add more milk if mixture is stiff.

Place in a lamington tin (flat tin approximately 30 cm by 20 cm), lined and greased well. Bake in a moderate oven 30 to 35 minutes.

Cool completely, then cut into even squares. Dip into Lamington Icing (see below), drain and roll in coconut. Lamingtons can be served with or without whipped cream. To add cream simply slice baked lamingtons and add a spoonful of whipped cream, and jam to decorate.

Lamington Icing
8 ounces powdered sugar (icing sugar)
2 Tablespoons cocoa powder
1 teaspoon butter, softened
1 cup of warm water

Blend icing sugar, cocoa, butter and a small amount of water to form a paste. Slowly add remaining water until it has a glaze consistency.

LUARNA DUNCAN, WODONGA, AUSTRALIA

Lamingtons with cream from Wodonga, Australia

PAVLOVA (PAV)

This is the most popular dessert at any Australian barbeque. A very simple recipe, but a favourite. Read *Possum Magic* by Mem Fox to see this Aussie treat. You can make larger or smaller versions – generally add 1/4 cup sugar per egg white. This particular recipe is one my Mum has modified over the years – a lot of recipe books include lemon and vinegar and different flour.

6 large egg whites, room temperature
1 1/2 cups of castor sugar (or superfine sugar)
1/2 Tablespoon corn flour
600 ml heavy whipping cream, whipped
Fresh strawberries, banana, passionfruit or chocolate for garnish

Beat egg whites until stiff on the highest beater setting. Slowly add sugar and corn flour. When mixed, put onto a lined flat baking sheet and mold into a round shape approximately 5 cm high. Use a knife or a spatula to peak edges.

Bake in a very slow oven for at least 2 hours. Pavlova should have a firm crust on the outside and a soft meringue on the inside. It should remain light in color. If it appears a pale brown, the oven may be too hot.

When the pavlova is completely cooled, carefully spoon whipped cream on top of pavlova shell. Decorate with fruit or chocolate. Best eaten the same day it is made.

Luarna Duncan, Wodonga, Australia

AUSTRALIAN SODA BISCUITS

These are traditionally called ANZAC biscuits: ANZAC stands for Australian New Zealand Army Corps. These biscuits are part of Australia's history. Baked for the soldiers during World War I, these biscuits keep well (notice the absence of eggs) and are great dunked in a cup of tea.

This recipe comes from my grandmother and it is an old farm favorite. They are great for school lunch boxes and afternoon tea. I personally love them hot out of the oven – mine never have a chance to cool!

1 cup flour
1 cup sugar
1 cup coconut
1 cup rolled oats
1/2 cup butter
2 Tablespoons golden syrup (a dark, thick syrup)*
3 Tablespoons boiling water
2 teaspoons baking soda

Combine all dry ingredients except soda. Melt butter and syrup. When melted, add water and soda and quickly pour over dry ingredients. Place spoon-sized piles on a well greased baking sheet and bake in a slow oven for 20 minutes.

Biscuits will spread. They will be golden brown and slightly soft when removed from the oven. They do become crispy as they cool.

LUARNA DUNCAN, WODONGA, AUSTRALIA

*Editor's Note: Golden syrup is widely available in Europe and Western Canada, but outside of Louisiana (where it's used in Cajun cooking) and specialty grocers, it may be hard to find in the rest of North America. If you're stuck, it is similar to honey, corn syrup and maple syrup so feel free to experiment accordingly.

Fiji

Modern Fijian cuisine is a unique compilation of indigenous cuisine blended with Indian, Chinese and European cuisines. One style of cooking, present in pre-colonial times and still used today, is the lovo, an oven created by lining a deep pit in the ground with stones and placing a fire in it. When the stones are hot, food is wrapped and placed in the pit, and soil is placed on top.

FISH AND LOLO (COCONUT MILK)

In Fiji, cooks will use whatever they have on hand, and whatever fish happened to be caught that day, so this recipe allows for a lot of variety and options: the amounts listed in the recipe are simply a guide, they can be adjusted to your own taste. You can use any kind of bony fish for this recipe, such as tilapia, milk fish, whole salmon, or smoked fish works well too. Lobster, crab legs, mussels and shrimp are awesome with this – it is all good. Enjoy, and as they say in Fiji, na kakana sa vakarau tu qo, vinaka vaka levu na kakana (the food is prepared so eat, thank you very much for the food).

Fresh whole fish or seafood, enough for a large group
1/2 cup olive oil or mustard seed oil, if frying fish
1 cup seasoned flour (flour mixed with pepper, roasted pepper and garlic spice, or other seafood or fish seasoning), if frying fish
2 Tablespoons olive oil
1 onion, chopped
2 cloves garlic, chopped
1 1-inch piece fresh ginger, chopped
1-2 cans coconut milk (my favorite is "AROY-D")
2 cups chopped cabbage
2 fresh tomatoes, chopped
salt and pepper to taste
1 Tablespoon fresh lemon juice
1 Tablespoon red curry spice and/or minced fresh hot pepper (optional)
1 cup Shanghai bok choy (mini bok choys), leaves separated

Descale the fish by soaking it in lukewarm water, just enough to cover the fish. Then use a fork and pull it upwards against the grain of the fish scales – you should be able to get most of them off without a lot of effort. At this point you can either fry the fish with just a little seasoned flour or add it directly to the pot. If you add it directly to the pot, skip the following step.

Heat oil in large sauté pan. Place seasoned flour in pie plate or other rimmed plate. Dredge the fish in flour mixture and fry it.

Add fish to a saucepan with remaining oil and onion, garlic and ginger. Blend together, then add coconut milk. Add cabbage, tomatoes, lemon juice, curry spice or hot pepper, if using, and season with salt and pepper. Cook everything on medium heat until fish is flaky: when it is almost done, turn heat down to low and add bok choy leaves.

Serve with a side bowl for everyone to put bones into. Keep the bones for the garden to fertilize your veggies, trees or flowers – works great!

LOLOMA LEVU THE KETECA MATAVUVALE (LOTS OF LOVE FROM THE KETECA FAMILY)

TANNIS KETECA, CALGARY, ALBERTA

EUROPE

England and Ireland

England and Ireland's cuisines today are remarkably similar to that of America, if only in spirit, because the same food trends have hit here as well: slow cooking, organic food, celebrity chefs, heightened concerns about health and obesity in the face of expanding fast food chains, and an interest in adopting the ingredients and dishes of other countries such as Italy, China, India and the Americas. A renewed commitment to excellence in ingredients and a spirit of innovation is improving the reputation for their cuisines, particularly in restaurants.

Traditionally, English cuisine focused on slow-cooked meats, sausages, fish, vegetables, and cheeses. Coffee and tea have played a prominent role in the English diet as well. Indeed, coffee houses began popping up in the 17th century, and became known as "penny universities" (the coffee was a penny, and people gathered here to exchange ideas and information). One of the first to start up is still going strong: Edward Lloyd opened his in 1688 – most people know it today as the insurance company Lloyd's of London.

SHEPHERD'S PIE

When I was young my mother would make this wonderful hearty dinner, especially in the cold winter months. She would often serve it with garden peas which I have continued the trend. It's an English favorite and certainly our family one! Even now my children's eyes light up when they ask "mum, what's for tea" and I reply "Shepherds Pie"!!

1 medium onion, chopped
2 teaspoons oil or fat
1/2 pound lean ground beef
Drop of red wine or beer (optional)
4 teaspoons tomato ketchup (optional)
2 shakes of Worcester sauce
1 beef stock cube
1 cup water
4-6 medium potatoes
4 carrots, sliced
1 ounce butter
Grated cheese (optional)
2 sliced tomatoes (optional)

Put the oil or fat in a frying pan and fry the onion and carrots gently for 4 to 5 minutes. Add the meat, and continue to fry gently, stirring all the time, until the meat has turned brown (approximately 5 minutes). Add the wine or beer, Worcester sauce, ketchup, stock cube and water. Stir well. Bring to a boil, then reduce heat and simmer for 20 – 30 minutes (stirring occasionally) until the meat is tender.

Meanwhile, peel the potatoes and cut into evenly-sized pieces. Cook in boiling, salted water for 15 - 20 minutes until soft. Drain and mash potatoes adding the butter until creamy.

Pour the meat mixture into an oven-proof dish, cover with the mashed potato and fork down smoothly. Sprinkle grated cheese over the potato (if desired) and place slices of tomato on top. Grill for a couple of minutes until golden brown. Serve with garden peas. Enjoy!

LORRAINE GREY, LONDON, ENGLAND AND CALGARY, ALBERTA

IRISH SODA BREAD – NIEMUR STYLE

Traditional Irish soda bread uses buttermilk instead of sour cream, and is baked in a round shape with a cross shape scored into the top. This version accounts for the fact that I never have buttermilk on hand, and my sweet tooth demands a little extra kick so yes, the cinnamon sugar is wholly inauthentic – but darn tasty –in a way this bread is almost a cross between Irish soda bread and sour cream pound cake. Mmmm….

5 cups flour
1 cup sugar
1 Tablespoon baking powder
1 teaspoon baking soda
1/2 teaspoon salt
4 eggs
2 cups sour cream
1/2 cup milk
2 Tablespoons butter, melted
1 Tablespoon cinnamon sugar (one scant Tablespoon sugar and 1/4 teaspoon cinnamon will do nicely)

Preheat oven to 325° and grease two 9 x 5 loaf pans. Blend flour, sugar, baking powder, baking soda and salt together in a large bowl. Stir eggs, sour cream and milk together in a small bowl: add wet ingredients to dry, and immediately spoon dough into prepared pans. Bake for one hour. As soon as bread is out of the oven, brush with melted butter and sprinkle with cinnamon sugar.

France

What can be said about French cooking that hasn't already been said? This is, after all, the country that brought the words café, vinegar, bistro, hors d'oeuvres, roux, and others into our lexicon. It is the home of the first restaurant and the source of the phrase "you are what you eat." It is where Julia Child cut her culinary chops and where Dom Perignon created Champagne. While its cuisine is not as old as that of Italy or China, France has, through the centuries, fostered a love of food and appreciation of fresh, local ingredients, skilled preparation techniques, and regional specialties. The fact that France happens to be Europe's largest agricultural producer doesn't hurt, either.

A brief history is in order: in 1533, Catherine de Medici arrived in Paris, bringing her Italian cooks with her to France, and married Henry II. Later, her cousin Marie married Henry IV and brought her chefs as well. The Italian contingents introduced new ingredients, including artichokes and truffles, and new approaches to cooking which French cooks adopted and continued to develop long after Henry's reign. Recipes became standardized. Years later, after the French Revolution, the royal chefs that were lucky enough to escape the guillotine began working in restaurants in unprecedented numbers, bringing the same skill and expertise to the people.

At the beginning of the 19th century, the French government offered an award of 12,000 francs to anyone who could come up with a solution for feeding soldiers that would both transport and preserve food. This challenge was answered by confectioner Nicolas Appert, who tinkered in his kitchen and came up with the equivalent of today's glass canning jars, which then led to the development of the aluminum can.

The 19th and early 20th centuries saw the rise of perhaps the original celebrity chefs. Jean-Antoine Carême, Escoffier and Prosper Montagne, author of the definitive *Larousse Gastronomique*, cooked for royalty and published books that became the authority on French cooking. Today these names are as well known in France as any other major historical figure.

Later, in reaction to the fat-laden recipes of formal haute cuisine, the trend of "nouvelle cuisine" appeared in the 1970s, with famed chef Paul Bocuse leading the charge. It favored fresh ingredients of the highest quality. Today most find a balance between the two and more attention is paid to regional cuisine, quality of ingredients, and techniques to enhance that natural flavor of every food.

To host a formal French dinner party, be sure to serve your food in courses: you could even print out a menu for your guests, if you so choose, to point out the name of each course. Note that entrées are not the main meal, as they are in North America, but simply the "first course." The order of your courses would be as follows:

- Apéritif
- Hors d'oeuvre or Appetizer
- Entrée or "first course"
- Main Course
- Salad

- Cheese
- Dessert or Fruit
- Coffee
- Digestif or after dinner drink

You wouldn't necessarily need to include every course – if you're hosting a more casual, homey affair you could offer a simple appetizer, followed by Cindy's Lamb and Lentil Stew, and then a simple dessert. Indeed, most of the recipes in this section actually reflect France's *cuisine bourgeoise*, or the home cooking that most French people eat on a regular basis – comfort food, you might say, versus the white-tablecloth, multiple-forks affair that is associated with haute cuisine.

Regardless of your style of dinner party, you don't have to invest in expensive wines, but wine should be included. Wine is consumed daily in France – to eat French food without wine would be akin to, well, a baseball game with no hot dogs! Be sure to chill your white wines ahead of time, and allow red wines to breathe at least one hour. A common misconception is that red wine can be served at room temperature – even if that's 75° or warmer. Instead, you should put a slight chill on the red wine since "room temperature" in French chateaux, back in the day, was a whole lot cooler – closer to 60 - 65° Fahrenheit.

RICE SALAD NIÇOISE

Not nearly as fancy as the plated "Salad Niçoise" from France, but in my opinion, even better. For a quick and easy summer meal, throw the rice in the rice cooker in the morning. I LOVE my rice cooker – it's an addition from our years at family housing at the University of Colorado in Boulder. Another couple, from Peru, introduced us to it, and we've never gone back to simmering rice on the stove.

3 cups cooked rice (white or brown)
1 diced red bell pepper
1 diced green bell pepper

1 diced tomato

1 6 ounce can tuna

1 can garbanzo beans (chickpeas), drained - optional

1 clove minced garlic

1/3 cup chopped fresh parsley

1/2 cup vinaigrette

Toss everything together in a big bowl, and dinner's in the fridge waiting for you at the end of the day.

CINDY LOZA, MARION, IOWA

PAN BAGNAT

This is a fabulous picnic take-along! I've also varied the theme by using other ingredients, such as banana peppers or an artichoke tapenade. I've also added goat cheese and have tried it with leftover sautéed veggies. My husband Kieran loves it (so does my son Henry!), and I like to fix it because it's a snap to put together in the morning, and there it is, all ready for you at the end of the day....

I usually cut the anchovy by half, as I'm not a huge fan of anchovies, but the beautiful thing is that you can mix and match to your heart's delight (remember Garanimals?). The Provençal name of this sandwich means "moist bread." If you're really feeling French, don't forget to pack the wine in your picnic basket!

1/2 cup olive oil

2 garlic cloves, minced

1 loaf sourdough bread, cut lengthwise

2 6-ounce cans solid white tuna, well drained

2 small red onion, very thinly sliced

4 large tomatoes, cut into 1/4 inch slices

1 2-ounce can anchovies (I use half), drained, chopped

2 Tablespoons drained capers

14 ounce jar roasted red peppers, well drained
1/2 cup chopped, pitted Kalamata olives or black olive tapenade

Mix oil and garlic in bowl. Hollow out inside of both bread halves, leaving 1/2 inch-thick sides. Brush insides of bread halves with garlic oil.

Spread tuna evenly over bottom half. Top with onion, then tomatoes, pressing down to compact. Sprinkle anchovies and capers over, pressing to adhere. Layer peppers over, then olives. Top with remaining bread half and press together.

Wrap tightly in plastic wrap or foil. Refrigerate at least 2 hours and up to 1 day. Cut bread crosswise into pieces and serve.

LISA MALONEY, BOULDER, COLORADO

LAMB AND LENTIL STEW

This recipe is "hats off" to my sister Cindy. She gave it to me, and I've literally made it for every occasion possible; from a dish to pass, to a "new baby" meal, to sharing a simple meal with mom and dad while grieving Mary Williams. Makes you feel good, even if you make it in the summer. It's really pretty simple to prepare, and packs a ton of nutrients. And the flavor, oi vey!! Kids love it because the prunes or figs add a certain sweetness, and the lentils are full of good stuff for you. It's a comforting dish, reheats the next day with even more flavor, and travels easily. Furthermore, it does well in the microwave and is even delicious cold. With a fresh salad and a loaf of good bread, you can't ask for much more. Kind of like being in France, where the recipe originated.... Thanks, Cindy and Lionel, for another outstanding epicurean delight!

1 Tablespoon olive oil
1 Tablespoon butter
1 pound lamb (I use shoulder chops) cut into small pieces

1 chopped onion

3 sliced celery ribs

2 sliced carrots

2 chopped garlic cloves

1 Tablespoon flour

2 cups vegetable or beef broth

1 cup pitted prunes or figs, cut into 1/2 inch dice

1/2 cup French green lentils (*not* regular brown lentils!)

4 sprigs fresh thyme or 1/2 teaspoon dried

salt and pepper to taste

Heat oil and butter in Dutch oven or big soup pan, and brown lamb on all sides. Remove meat; set aside. Add onion to pan, and cook slowly until soft but not brown, then add celery, carrot and garlic. Cook 2-3 minutes more.

Stir flour into vegetables, cook 1-2 minutes then gradually add the broth, stirring the bottom to scrape up any bits. Bring to a boil; add prunes (or figs, equally delicious) and lentils; simmer 3 minutes.

Return lamb to casserole and add thyme, salt and pepper. Put all of it in a glass baking dish (round, if possible) in preheated 325° oven for 1 1/2 to 2 hours, depending on your oven. Season to taste with salt and pepper (I haven't had to do this yet, and I've made it 15 times!)

LISA MALONEY, BOULDER, COLORADO

KIR

This French mixed drink became popular in America in the 1970s. It is enjoyed in France in an outdoor café at any hour of day, or as an aperitif before lunch or dinner. The wine most used is white Burgundy, but any chilled dry white wine will work. For special occasions champagne may be substituted for the wine: the name then changes to Kir Royale, one of many variations on the original.

Combine 1/2 cup chilled wine with 1 Tablespoon crème de cassis in a wine glass. If you wish you may add ice and/or sparkling water.

Cranberry Kir Royale

Put 2 Tablespoons cranberry juice and 1 Tablespoon crème de cassis in a champagne flute and add 1/4 cup of champagne.

SHERYL TUSCH, HUDSONVILLE, MICHIGAN

Editor's Note: The word *kir* actually comes from the name of the apéritif's most ardent advocate. When sales of crème de cassis lagged after World War II, Félix Kir, the mayor of Dijon in Burgundy, promoted the local product whenever possible and a *vin blanc cassis* became known simply as a *kir*.

SOLE MEUNIÈRE

Any dish that has the name *meunière* attached to it will always have flour in the recipe, since the meunière, in the days before large-scale flour production, was the miller's wife. Kudos to the French for honoring the hard work that wives put in, too!

This dish is a standard of French cooking and a snap to put together at the last minute. The oil helps prevent the butter from burning, but take care not to allow your pan to smoke.

    4 fillets of sole
    1/2 cup flour
    6 Tablespoons butter
    1 Tablespoon vegetable oil
    1 lemon, sliced lengthwise, each half cut in 1/4" slices
    2 Tablespoons fresh lemon juice
    1/4 cup minced fresh parsley

Dredge fillets in flour. Heat 3 Tablespoons of the butter, and oil, in large sauté pan and add fillets, cooking for 3-5 minutes or until browned. Remove fillets to serving plate and keep warm. Add remaining butter to pan, allow it to melt and sizzle for one minute, then add lemon slices, lemon juice and parsley. Stir everything together quickly in pan, then drizzle over fish.

CHICKEN WITH 40 CLOVES OF GARLIC

This dish is to French cooking what apple pie is to American baking – a classic that is here to stay. The job is made infinitely easier by purchasing pre-peeled garlic cloves. To quickly remove thyme leaves from sprigs, run forefinger and thumb down the sprig from top to bottom and the leaves will fall off. One final tip – the browning process is not necessary, but adds a nice color and texture to the chicken. If you're in a hurry, you can go right to the oven.

6-7 pounds of chicken pieces, bone-in
1/4 cup vegetable oil
1 onion, chopped
4 ribs of celery, chopped in 1 inch pieces
1/4 cup fresh parsley, chopped
10 sprigs fresh thyme, and one bunch for garnish
1/2 cup dry white wine
1/2 cup chicken stock
1/2 teaspoon Kosher salt
1/4 teaspoon ground black pepper
40 cloves of garlic, peeled
1 baguette or loaf of crusty bread

In large pan, heat oil and brown chicken pieces briefly and set aside. Preheat oven to 350°. Place onion and celery in the bottom of a large casserole or Dutch oven. Top with parsley and thyme. Place chicken pieces on top, add wine and stock, and sprinkle salt and pepper over chicken pieces. Tuck garlic cloves among the chicken pieces, seal the pan with aluminum foil, and place lid on top of foil. Roast for 1 1/2 hours, or until meat juices run clear. Place chicken on a platter and garnish with extra thyme. Remove garlic cloves and serve separately as a spread for bread.

POMMES PARMENTIER

When the humble potato jumped the pond from South America to Europe, diners in France were reluctant to try it out for many years. But scientist Antoine-Augustin Parmentier, having eaten them as a prisoner of war in Prussia, was determined to convince his countrymen of its value. Demonstrating a keen insight into human nature, he planted a very public garden of potatoes and had armed soldiers guard the plantings during the day. At night the soldiers left, and one by one the potatoes disappeared. After a while, the citizens decided those tubers were okay after all. To honor the man who persuaded France to try potatoes, we now have this classic French recipe. Likewise, a creamy potato soup is known in France as potage Parmentier.

1/4 cup olive oil
6 medium potatoes, neatly diced into 1/2" cubes
2 strips bacon, pre-cooked
2 garlic cloves, minced
1 Tablespoon minced fresh parsley
salt and pepper to taste

Heat oil in large sauté pan. Add potatoes and cook, stirring occasionally, until they begin to brown. Add bacon and garlic and stir through 2 minutes more. Remove from heat, add parsley, salt and pepper. Serve hot.

Austria, Germany and Switzerland

These western European countries reflect the bounty that surrounds them, with many dishes featuring meat, eggs and butter. With so many rich ingredients available, pastries and other baked goods have become works of art here: indeed, pastry chefs from these countries are highly sought after, and Salzburg, Austria can take the prize for inventing meringue. Sachertorte was invented in Vienna in 1832, and Vienna is also the origin of what is now referred to as Danish pastry (the Danes call it wienerbrod, or Viennese bread). Throw in Nina's rice pudding, some Swiss chocolate, and German Schwarzwälder Kirschtorte (Black Forest Torte) and you've got yourself a nice little dessert tasting party!

While at first one may assume these countries did not have the same impact on global cuisine as say, France, Persia or China, there are elements of what we consider traditional American cuisine that come directly from the region. Hamburgers, frankfurters, roasted meat and potatoes, Christmas cookies, and gingerbread houses were all inherited from Germany.

STOLLEN

My grandma would make this every Christmas Eve – she'd usually make two so that we'd have one with dinner, and have another one for Christmas Day breakfast. She'd always decorate it with a delicious icing, topped with Technicolor red and green maraschino cherries. I've omitted them from this recipe, but if you like to go all out with your Christmas colors, by all means add the cherries!

Stollen, a yeast-raised sweet bread, originates from Germany, where it is traditionally served at Christmastime (the finished product said to resemble the swaddled baby Jesus). The first mention of it comes from a Dresden document dated 1474, so as recipes go this one has a proven track record. Every year Dresden celebrates with a stollenfest, honoring the days when their king, August the Strong, had a giant stollen made to serve all his subjects. The tradition continues, and in 2000 Dresden broke the Guinness World Record for the largest stollen, which weighed in at just 4.2 tons.

Stollen comes in several varieties – sometimes it is stuffed with a mixture of almond paste and sugar, and sometimes other fruits and nuts are used. Feel free to play around with the add-ins.

1 1/2 cups milk
1/2 cup white sugar
3/4 cup butter
1/2 teaspoon salt
3 eggs
5 1/2 - 6 cups all-purpose flour
1 0.25-ounce packet or 2 1/4 teaspoons active dry yeast
1/2 teaspoon ground cardamom
1 cup raisins
1/2 cup chopped apricots
1 teaspoon vegetable oil (or more if needed)
1/4 cup melted butter

1 cup powdered sugar
1 Tablespoon milk
1/4 teaspoon almond extract

Place butter and milk in a small pan over low-medium heat, melting the butter and scalding the milk. Pour into a large bowl, add sugar and salt, and cool to lukewarm. Add eggs and stir. Quickly mix in yeast then 3 cups of flour, cover and let it rise until doubled, about 30 minutes.

Add cardamom, raisins, apricots, and 2 cups of flour. Set on floured work surface and knead for 5 minutes, adding flour as needed to create a soft dough. Cover dough lightly with vegetable oil, and let rise in a bowl covered with a clean dishtowel.

After dough has risen, cut into 3 pieces. Roll each into an oval, brush with melted butter, and fold in half lengthwise. Put on greased baking sheet, cover, and let rise until doubled again. Preheat oven to 375°.

Bake loaves for 25 minutes. Remove to rack. Stir powdered sugar, milk and almond extract together. When loaves have completely cooled, drizzle with powdered sugar glaze.

REISAUFLAUF (BAKED RICE PUDDING)

I got this recipe from dear old Frau Gasteiger in Bavaria, Germany. We were in Germany in the summer of 2006 visiting the dairy farm that I grew up on. This recipe always takes me back to my childhood and the yummy smells of Frau Gasteiger's kitchen, and my magical childhood growing up on a farm in the Bavarian Alps.

Simmer for 45 minutes on very low heat:
6 1/2 cups milk

2 cups rice

In separate bowl, mix until frothy:
1/2 cup softened butter
4 egg yolks
3/4 – 1 cup sugar, depending on sweetness desired
2 teaspoons vanilla or lemon juice
1 cup raisins (optional)

Beat egg whites in separate bowl.

Fold together rice mixture, butter mixture and egg whites. Pour in buttered casserole dish and bake at 375° for 40 minutes. Yummy by itself, or with fruit or whipped cream.

NINA SHURTS, BANKS, OREGON

LENTIL WITH LEMON SOUP

We used to make this soup frequently during the winter when we were living in Geneva, Switzerland and I was working at the World Health Organization. We always made it without bacon:

2 Tablespoons olive oil
1 1/2 cups dried lentils, rinsed
1 cup chopped onion
2 medium carrots, sliced
1 celery stalk, sliced
1 garlic clove, minced
6 cups water
1 teaspoon grated lemon peel
1 bay leaf
1 1/2 teaspoons salt

1 large potato, peeled, diced

3 Tablespoons lemon juice

1 teaspoon ground cumin

4 large Swiss chard leaves or fresh spinach leaves, shredded

Place olive oil in a 4-quart pot. (Optional: fry 2 bacon slices until crisp, drain on paper towels, save 2 Tablespoons bacon drippings, crumble bacon).

Add onion, carrots, celery and garlic to olive oil or reserved drippings in skillet. Saute until onion is tender. Add sauteed vegetables to lentils. Stir in water, lemon peel, bay leaf, salt and diced potato.Bring to a boil; reduce heat. Cover and simmer until lentils are tender—about 45 minutes. Stir in (bacon), lemon juice, cumin and Swiss chard or spinach. Makes 5 servings.

SANDRA ANDERSON, TUCSON, ARIZONA

Editor's Note: This soup has become our standard remedy when someone in our family has a cold. It's delicious, it's comforting, and between the lentils, garlic, lemon and Swiss chard, it's a nutritional powerhouse!

Greece

Think Greeks don't take their olive oil seriously? Aristotle, in his record of Athenian law, wrote that anyone who felled an olive tree and was found guilty of the crime would be sentenced to death. Yeesh. Things have mellowed since Aristotle's time, but Greeks still have much to be proud of when it comes to their cuisine. Olive oil, fish and seafood, grains and vegetables make up a large portion of the diet, earning it a reputation as one of the world's healthiest.

Greek *meze*, small dishes sometimes served as appetizers, include dolmades, or stuffed grape leaves, spanakopita, or spinach wrapped in phyllo pastry, or even a simple dish of cheese and olives.

My friend Maria, who contributed two recipes in this section, lives in New York but her parents and extended family are from the Greek island of Chios, which is the primary producer of mastic, an evergreen shrub that is cultivated for its resin which in turn is used as a flavoring for drinks, desserts and sauces, as well as other applications. The resin is also referred to quite poetically as "Chios tears."

GREEK MEATBALLS (KEFTEDAKIA)

Kefalotiri is a hard salty cheese made from either sheep or goat's milk, and was first developed in Greece during the Byzantine era.

  4 slices firm bread
  1 pound lean ground beef
  1 medium yellow onion, grated
  1/4 cup dry wine or vermouth
  1 large egg, beaten
  1 clove garlic, minced
  2 Tablespoons parsley, minced
  3 Tablespoons mint, minced or 1 teaspoon dried mint, crushed
  1 Tablespoon grated Kefalotiri or Romano cheese
  1/2 teaspoon oregano
  salt and pepper to taste

Moisten bread with water and squeeze dry. Place in a medium sized bowl. Add remaining ingredients and mix. Season with salt and pepper. Allow mixture to rest in the refrigerator to allow flavors to "marry."

Roll into small balls. Broil, turning once. Makes 25 meatballs.
MARIA LOS, NEW YORK, NEW YORK

EGGPLANT AND MEAT CASSEROLE WITH BECHAMEL SAUCE (MOUSSAKA)

Bechamel Sauce:
1/2 cup butter or margarine
1/2 cup flour
4 cups scalded milk
1/8 teaspoon nutmeg

salt and pepper to taste
4 large eggs
paprika for garnish

Melt the butter in a heavy 4 quart saucepan. Add the flour and cook over medium heat for 10 minutes, stirring constantly. Slowly add 2 cups of the scalded milk and stir with a whisk until smooth. Add the nutmeg and season with salt and pepper. Remove from heat.

Beat the eggs in a blender or processor until frothy. With the machine running, gradually add the remaining 2 cups of scalded milk. Slowly return the contents of the blender or processor to the saucepan, stirring constantly until thickened. Remove from the heat and set aside.

Casserole:
4 large ripe eggplants (about 5 pounds)
1 cup vegetable oil (for brushing eggplant slices)
2 Tablespoons olive or vegetable oil
2 yellow onions, grated
1 clove garlic, minced
2 ribs of celery, minced
3 pounds lean ground beef
1 cup parsley, minced
1/2 teaspoon cinnamon
1/4 teaspoon nutmeg
1/4 teaspoon allspice
1 16-ounce can of tomato sauce
1/2 cup dry wine
salt and pepper to taste
1/3 cup bread crumbs
2/3 cup grated Kefalotiri or Romano cheese

Peel the eggplants and cut lengthwise into 1/2 inch slices. Lightly brush each side with oil on both sides. Lay on foil-lined cookie sheets and broil, turning once, until brown and tender. Set aside.

Heat the 2 Tablespoons of oil in a 10 inch non-stick skillet and sauté the onion, garlic and celery until the onion is tender but not brown. Add the meat and brown thoroughly. Pour off and discard any excess fat from the skillet. Add the parsley, spices, tomato sauce and wine. Simmer over medium heat for 15 minutes or until most of the liquid is absorbed. Season with salt and pepper. The mixture should be thick. Set aside.

To assemble the casserole: grease a 10 x 15 x 3 inch baking pan. Sprinkle the pan with bread crumbs. Layer 1/2 of the eggplant slices over the bottom of the pan, overlapping if necessary. Sprinkle with salt and pepper and 1/3 cup of the grated cheese. Spread the meat mixture over the cheese and pat down with a spatula to make a smooth, flat layer. Top with the remaining eggplant slices. Season with salt and pepper, and add another 1/3 cup of cheese. Top with a thick layer of béchamel sauce.

Make in a preheated 375° oven for 45 minutes or until the béchamel is golden brown and puffy. Remove from the oven and run a knife around the edge of the pan to free the crust from the pan. Allow moussaka to rest for 15 minutes. Cut into squares and serve. Makes 12 entrée or 24 buffet servings.

Maria Los, New York, New York

GREEK FAJITAS

This is by no means a traditional Greek recipe, but rather the result of one day wanting chicken souvlaki and lacking the pita bread. The result was a wildly popular dish that I get requests for over and over again. Serve with fattoush or tabbouleh salad and fresh fruit for a refreshing summer dinner. Let everyone assemble the fajitas according to their tastes, and supply plenty of napkins!

Serves 4

1 package of 8-10 flour tortillas
4-6 chicken breast halves
1 bottle Greek vinaigrette dressing
1 red onion, sliced thin
1 cucumber, sliced thin
4 Roma tomatoes, sliced thin
1 cup crumbled Feta cheese

Marinate chicken breasts in 1/2 bottle of Greek vinaigrette for 1- 3 hours. Grill on medium-high heat until done, turning once or twice. Meanwhile, wrap entire package of tortillas in aluminum foil and warm in a 350° oven for 10 minutes.

Assemble the onion, cucumber and tomato slices on a platter, and place in the middle of the table with the Feta cheese and remaining vinaigrette. When the chicken is done, slice into strips. Remove tortillas from the oven and put all the ingredients on the table.

Italy – Calabria

Italy, perhaps more than any other country, maintains strong regional identities, in its cuisine and culture. Dialects vary so widely from region to region, they may as well be separate languages. So too do the cuisines of Italy vary from region to region. For this reason I will not attempt to recreate the multitudes of regional Italian cuisines – that would not just be another book, it would be a multi-volume set! Instead we will focus on the southern region of Calabria.

The steep hillside homes of Calabria, in Italy.

From Calabria to Canada

One of our contributing writers, now living in Calgary, originally hails from Christina Lake, British Columbia. Her parents moved to Canada from the Calabria region of Italy, and like other immigrants, brought recipes that had to be adapted to the their new surroundings. Some recipes call for smoked paprika, which I have used here as close a substitute as possible for a particular Calabrese dried chili (peperoncino) that flavors many of the dishes in that region.

If you can visualize the boot-shape of Italy, then Calabria is the toe of the boot that kicks Sicily. Early in its history, because of its vulnerable coastal position, the region endured occupation by the Greeks, Romans, Visigoths, Moors, Normans, Spanish and other invaders. It is a perfect example of how a region can absorb different cultures, not just in terms of cuisine but language as well. To wit: Albanians fled to Calabria in the 1400s, and today in the village of Castrovillari medieval Albanian is still the local language. Calabria's rugged coastline has prevented agricultural and industrial development, prompting many in the region to relocate for employment, although tourism is on the rise. Some foods do flourish here, however, particularly eggplant, figs, and the bergamot, a citrus fruit that is used in Earl Grey tea and in perfumes and soaps. The Greek wine Cirò, said by some to be the oldest wine in the world, is produced here as well. Indeed, the Greeks originally called this region "Enotria" or "Land of Wine" because they believed the terrain lent itself well to vineyards.

In terms of cuisine, vegetable dishes, cheeses, pasta, fish, and sausages made with the Calabrese chili are particularly popular. The sausages include capocollo, soppressata, and 'ndugghia, a pork-based sausage that comes from the French andouille. Many specialty foods are produced in this region, including porcini mushrooms, chestnuts, olive oil, and pecorino, caciocavallo, and provolone cheeses. Dried figs are a Calabrese specialty, and desserts featuring the fruit are served on special occasions. Calabria and Sicily both feature desserts with figs, raisins and almonds, revealing the influence of Middle Eastern cuisine.

MASTAZOLA

4 cups creamed honey
2 eggs
1 Tablespoon oil
1 teaspoon baking soda
flour – add until workable dough (about 4-5 cups)

Preheat oven to 350° and grease and flour cookie sheets. Mix all ingredients together. Sprinkle work surface, take 1/4 of the dough and and roll out to 1/4-1/2" thickness. Cut with cookie cutters or glass, and bake at for 10-15 minutes or until golden.

LINDA ABENANTE O'DONOGHUE, CALGARY, ALBERTA

Editor's Note: We should all be eating more honey! It has the same amount of antioxidants as spinach, oranges and strawberries (the darker the variety, the more antioxidants present), and some varieties even have antimicrobial qualities. Nature's antibiotic, as it were. And next time you make some mastazola, thank those bees for their cooperative effort: in its lifetime, a single bee will produce less than 1/10 of a teaspoon of honey.

ITALIAN STYLE PIZZA

One batch of pizza dough (see recipe)
2 ripe tomatoes
1/2 teaspoon salt
2 teaspoons oregano, divided
4 Tablespoons grated Parmesan cheese, divided
1/2 teaspoon ground black pepper
1/2 cup green pepper, diced
1 Tablespoon olive oil
1 cup shredded mozzarella cheese

Cut tomatoes in small chunks, sprinkle salt and 1 teaspoon oregano on top and put into a colander to drain for 5-10 minutes.

On pizza dough, sprinkle 2 Tablespoons Parmesan cheese, oregano, and pepper.

Then add green pepper, tomatoes, olive oil, remaining Parmesan, and 1/4 cup of mozzarella. Bake at 400° for 6-10 minutes. When pizza is almost cooked, add remaining mozzarella.

Linda Abenante O'Donoghue, Calgary, Alberta

PIZZA DOUGH I (FOR THREE ROUND PIZZAS)

3 cups flour
1 Tablespoon yeast
1 teaspoon salt
1 teaspoon of solid vegetable shortening
1 beaten egg
1 1/4 cups water

Combine dry ingredients in a large mixing bowl. Add shortening, using a pastry cutter or hands to mix in. Make a well with the ingredients, and add egg and water in the middle. Mix and form a ball. Allow dough to rest for fifteen minutes, then roll out dough for pizza. Bake at 375° for about 15-20 minutes.

LINDA ABENANTE O'DONOGHUE, CALGARY, ALBERTA

PIZZA DOUGH II

1 teaspoon sugar
1 cup warm water
1 Tablespoon yeast
3 cups flour
1 teaspoon salt
2 Tablespoons olive oil

Put sugar in warm water, sprinkle yeast on surface. Let sit for ten minutes or until foamy. Meanwhile, combine salt and flour. Stir oil into yeast mixture, then stir in 1/2 of flour mixture. Gradually add flour mixture until in a slightly sticky ball. Knead for five minutes and cut dough in half. Cover with wax paper and rest ten minutes. Roll out in pans, and rest fifteen minutes. Bake at 350° for 16-18 minutes.

LINDA ABENANTE O'DONOGHUE, CALGARY, ALBERTA

GNOCCHI FOR FOUR

8 Russet potatoes, medium size
2 cups flour
1 Tablespoon olive oil
1 egg yolk
1 whole egg
Pasta Sauce (see recipe)

Bake potatoes at 350° with skins on until soft. Cut in half, scoop out potato and pass through potato ricer. On a large cutting board, put 1/2 cup of flour (sprinkled) and put potatoes on top. Make a well and add oil and eggs. Using a potato masher, mix potatoes with well contents. Add rest of flour a bit at a time and mix. Then knead dough until well mixed.

Fill a large saucepan with water and bring to a boil. Add salt. Cut sections of dough and roll out to a finger-sized snake. Cut into 1 inch pieces, roll with fingers, place on floured cookie sheet. Add to boiling, salted water a bit at a time and remove gently with slotted spoon. Serve with heated pasta sauce.

LINDA ABENANTE O'DONOGHUE, CALGARY, ALBERTA

MANICOTTI

1 1/2 Tablespoons butter
6 packed cups fresh spinach, washed and torn
1 – ounce tub of Ricotta cheese
12 large manicotti noodles
1 cup shredded mozzarella cheese
2 Tablespoons grated Parmesan cheese
1 Tablespoon chopped fresh parsley
Pinch of black pepper
2 eggs

Pasta Sauce (see below)

Cook manicotti noodles in a large stockpot to al dente. Meanwhile, melt butter in sauté pan and add spinach. Saute until spinach has wilted. Add into ricotta in a bowl, then add 1/2 cup of the mozzarella, Parmesan, black pepper, eggs and parsley, mix together. Stuff manicotti, put sauce on bottom of a pan and then on top of manicotti. Add remaining mozzarella on top. Bake 20 minutes at 350°.

LINDA ABENANTE O'DONOGHUE, CALGARY, ALBERTA

MEATBALLS

8 ounces lean ground beef
1 frozen hamburger bun, grated
3 Tablespoons Parmesan cheese
1 dash black pepper
1 dash garlic powder or garlic salt
1 teaspoon dried parsley
1 egg
Pasta Sauce (see recipe)

Add all ingredients except breadcrumbs to meat and mix well. Roll meatballs and roll them in breadcrumbs. Bake in oven for 10 minutes at 350-400°. Add meatballs to sauce and simmer for at least one hour.

LINDA ABENANTE O'DONOGHUE, CALGARY, ALBERTA

PASTA AND PEAS CALABRESE

1 Tablespoon olive oil
1 Tablespoon chopped onions
1 garlic clove, chopped

1 cup tomatoes – stew until tomatoes separate, or used canned stewed tomatoes
3/4 cup water
Salt and pepper to taste
1/4 teaspoon dried red pepper or smoked paprika
1/2 cup peas
2 cups cooked pasta

Heat oil in a saucepan on low-medium heat. Add onions and garlic and sauté for one minute, then add remaining ingredients. Serve on top of cooked pasta.

Linda Abenante O'Donoghue, Calgary, Alberta

PASTA AND PRAWNS WITH BROCCOLI

2 Tablespoons olive oil
1 cup chopped onions
4 cloves of garlic, minced
1 1/2 cups of sliced mushrooms
3/4 cup canned diced tomatoes
1/4 cup Pesto sauce, or more to taste
2 cups broccoli flowerets
1 bag of 31/40 count shrimp, thawed and peeled
2 Tablespoons freshly grated Parmesan cheese

Heat olive oil in sauté pan, and sauté onions, garlic, and mushrooms for ten minutes on low heat. Meanwhile, blanch broccoli in boiling water (no more than one minute). Add tomatoes, shrimp, pesto and broccoli to vegetables for five minutes, and add black pepper to taste. Sprinkle with Parmesan cheese and serve.

Linda Abenante O'Donoghue, Calgary, Alberta

Editor's Note: What Canadians think of as prawns, Americans would call shrimp. Note that this recipe and the one that follows use "prawns" in the title, but use what Americans would consider shrimp. If you use *prawns*, as in those large-scale gems, either recipe will work just as well but you'll need to adjust your cooking time accordingly.

PASTA SAUCE FOR MANICOTTI, MEATBALLS AND GNOCCHI

3 Tablespoons olive oil
1/4 cup chopped onions
2 garlic cloves, minced
2 cups canned tomatoes
2 cups tomato sauce
1 7-ounce can of tomato paste
2 cups water
1/2 teaspoon black pepper
1 teaspoon dried Italian seasoning
1 scant teaspoon salt

Heat oil in saucepan and add onions and garlic. Sauté for 1 minute and turn heat to low. Add tomatoes, sauce and mix. Add tomato paste, water, spices and salt. Bring to a boil then reduce heat to simmer lightly for one and a half hours.
LINDA ABENANTE O'DONOGHUE, CALGARY, ALBERTA

Editor's Note: This is the recipe for pasta sauce that comes from Calabria, so I would never think to alter in any way, but it is a very mild sauce. If you like to have a lot of "oomph" in your sauce, I would recommend doubling any or all of the onions, garlic, pepper and/or Italian seasoning – but the sauce is delicious just as it is.

PRAWNS FOR TWO

10-15 ready to eat shrimp
1 Tablespoon olive oil
1/2 clove garlic, minced
1 Tablespoon fresh parsley, chopped fine
Pinch black pepper
Pinch salt
2 Tablespoons dry breadcrumbs
1 lemon wedge

Rinse and dry prawns in paper towel. Put into bowl and combine all the ingredients in the order written. Mix together and refrigerate for five hours. When ready to serve, put prawns onto a pizza pan and broil for five minutes or less each side, until golden.

LINDA ABENANTE O'DONOGHUE, CALGARY, ALBERTA

CALABRESE STUFFING FOR TURKEY

1/4 cup olive oil
1 small onion
1 green pepper
1 small zucchini
1 can mushrooms
1 pound lean ground beef
1/2 cup chopped fresh parsley
2 cups dry breadcrumbs
1/2 cup freshly grated Parmesan cheese
2 eggs

Heat oil in sauté pan. Chop vegetables very fine, and cook in sauté pan until onion is tender. Salt and pepper to taste. Brown beef separately, and drain and allow to cool slightly. Mix everything in a large bowl, making sure beef is not too hot when mixing in the eggs.

Linda Abenante O'Donoghue, Calgary, Alberta

AUTOGRILL SALAD

This is the salad we had while touring Italy at the famous Autogrills placed along the roads in Italy, where you can get an espresso, gourmet groceries, baked goods, lunch or dinner and snacks for the road!

Spring greens and chopped romaine
1 can tuna in water, drained
tomato wedges
Kalamata or country olives
1 fresh buffalo mozzarella, small
blanched green beans or asparagus
dried oregano
good white wine vinegar
extra virgin olive oil

Start with the greens on a plate, then top with tuna, tomatoes, olives, mozzarella and beans or asparagus (it is nice to pile these last three in mounds all together). Sprinkle with oregano. Splash with vinegar and oil. Serves one.

Teri Mercier, Calgary, Alberta

The Netherlands

I am proud to call myself Dutch, and just look at a few who can say the same: social liberals in Amsterdam accepting of legalized narcotics, and conservative Midwestern Americans. Farmers in South Africa, and men, women and children who risked their lives to save Jews and others during World War II. Ruthless privateers who exploited entire populations to purchase nutmeg and then sell it at a 60,000% markup during the Age of Exploration, and innovative architects in modern Manhattan. Parents who tell their children about Sinter Klaas and his assistants who may or may not try to kidnap you on Christmas Eve, depending on how good you've been. How on God's green earth did we all spring from such a tiny place, a nation whose very existence is a modern miracle? Say what you will about our history as a colonial power, but the Dutch get the gold medal for engineering. Agriculture, industry and the arts thrive in a lowland area at or under sea level. Wonders never cease.

During the Age of Exploration, motivated by the money to be made by spices purchased in Asia, the Netherlands launched ships and established the Dutch East India Company. It had lasting influence on the cuisine of its former colony

Indonesia (which, conversely, has had influence on Dutch cuisine). Dutch cuisine can also be found in the Dutch Antilles islands of Aruba, Bonaire and Curaçao, known as the "ABC" islands. The city of Willemstad, on Curaçao, has recently been named as a UNESCO World Heritage site, in part for its colorful Dutch architecture.

The Dutch people I do know are the salt of the earth (oh, I had to use a food metaphor, didn't I?) and have provided the lion's share of the recipes here and in the Michigan section. Since this is the Netherlands section, though, and not the Dutch west Michigan section, I guarantee the following recipes are free of cream of mushroom soup. Eet smakelijk!

HERRING WITH APPLE AND CREAM SAUCE

At home our Dutch cuisine choices are limited, but herring is very popular in the Netherlands. We had trouble eating and enjoying the raw herring that was presented there. This recipe I first made for our French son-in-law, Lionel, who loves herring in wine sauce. It works well as an hors d'oeuvre served at the table before dinner.

2 Granny Smith apples, peeled, cored, and finely diced
1/2 onion, minced
11/2 cups of heavy cream
1 Tablespoon fresh chives, minced
1 Tablespoon fresh lemon juice
1 pound herring, marinated in wine, strained
1 bunch Bibb lettuce, washed, dried, leaves separated
1 tomato, sliced

In a medium bowl mix apples, onion, cream, chives and lemon juice. Mix. Add herring and mix in. Cover, refrigerate, and marinate overnight. On individual plates or one large one, put lettuce leaves, herring, and garnish with tomato slices.

Sheryl Tusch, Hudsonville, Michigan

HUTSPOT

This Dutch dish is tasty, but will have some lumps in it. Don't expect it to be exactly like creamy mashed potatoes.

6 onions, diced
6 carrots, diced
8 potatoes, peeled and cubed
2 – 5 Tablespoons butter
1/2 cup whole milk
1 teaspoon salt or more to taste
1 teaspoon ground black pepper or more to taste

Boil onions and carrots. Drain. Boil potatoes, drain and dry thoroughly, add onions and carrots and mash fine. Add salt and pepper, butter and milk. Stew all together until heated through and serve. Apples may be substituted for the carrots.

Sheryl Tusch, Hudsonville, Michigan

Editor's Note: Hutspot is eaten every October 3 in the Netherlands, to commemorate the holiday of Leiden Ontzet. On this day in 1574, Dutch forces liberated the city of Leiden. It had been under siege by Spanish troops during the Eighty Years' War when the Dutch broke the dams, flooding the countryside and sending the Spaniards running. Residents of Leiden, desperate for food, found stores of cooked potatoes among the things the Spanish had quickly left behind. From this story comes the recipe for hutspot, which probably originally included parsnips as well. During the Nazi occupation of World War II, hutspot was a symbol for freedom from oppression since its main ingredients, root vegetables, were grown underground and could therefore be kept hidden from enemy forces.

KOOLMOES (CABBAGE AND POTATOES)

This is another Dutch recipe using simple ingredients available on the farm. It is nutritious and filling and inexpensive.

    8 medium potatoes, peeled
    1 head of cabbage
    4 Tablespoons butter
    salt and pepper
    1/2 cup cream

Boil potatoes and drain. Shred and boil cabbage and drain. Mash together, add butter and season. If mixture is dry, add 1/2 cup cream. Apples may be substituted for the cabbage.

SHERYL TUSCH, HUDSONVILLE, MICHIGAN

MOUSE

This is a Dutch dish that sounds strange, but the flavors and textures on the served plate are wonderful. I'm not sure where the title comes from; I only know it as "mouse."

    8 or 9 potatoes
    2 cans of kale and the juice
    1 mettwurst, cut into 3 inch pieces
    2 onions
    3 Tablespoons butter

Boil potatoes, onions, and mettwurst until potatoes are done. Drain, keeping 1 cup of liquid. Remove meat. Mash the potatoes and onions. Add a little of the saved liquid (or use milk). Add butter and kale with juice. Add more liquid, if needed. Serve with the mettwurst, applesauce, and pickles.

SHERYL TUSCH, HUDSONVILLE, MICHIGAN

Denmark, Finland, Norway and Sweden

As early as the 9th century Vikings from Scandinavia launched raids on their European neighbors, motivated in part by limited resources of food. While the seas provided an abundance of fish, the northern climate meant a limited growing season and people were left to use what was available, including wild game. It is telling that in Valhalla, the Viking equivalent of Heaven, a wild boar would be served, consumed, and then appear whole again the next night.

Not surprisingly, much of Scandinavian food today still revolves around fish, game, seafood, and grains and vegetables that can tolerate a colder climate. Combine these with ingredients like pepper, dill, caraway seed, allspice, bay leaves, berries, dark breads, pancakes, root vegetables, sweet cream and sour cream, and cheeses and you have the foundation of these northern cuisines.

The four countries that comprise Scandinavia certainly do have individual culinary identities: for example, Denmark, which is also closely tied to the rest of

Europe, is more temperate and grows a wider variety of vegetables and grains. Finland, bordering Russia, shares many of its neighbor's culinary traditions, including blini, and the Samis or Lapps of northern Finland to this day use the reindeer much like the Prairie Indians used bison in North America – nothing is wasted (in Alberta I've heard the bison referred to as the "walking Wal-Mart").

Norway takes much of its cuisine from the sea, and farm wives for years have continued a tradition of hanging baskets filled with bread, butter and sausages from the eaves of their storehouse for any hungry passersby. Sweden is the only country of the four that developed a formal court cuisine; veal Oscar is named for King Oscar II, who liked his veal topped with asparagus and hollandaise sauce.

If you'd like to host a Scandanavian potluck or dinner party, you could recreate the smorgasbord, a series of dishes that always starts with herring. Each course is served on top of buttered black (rye) bread, or smorrebroet.

AEBLESKIVERS TWO WAYS

As a young child, I grew up going to Grayling, Michigan for the summers. My great-great grandfather came over from Sweden and settled there. He built three family cabins that we still have and use today. My grandmother used to make this for us when we would be staying with her. We had it as a dessert, despite the name "pancake." We would continue this family tradition each summer.

Grandma's Recipe

> 1/2 pint sour cream
> 1 cup flour
> 1/2 teaspoon baking soda
> 1/4 cup sugar
> 3 egg whites, beaten stiff

Blend first four ingredients together. Beat egg whites until stiff and fold into batter. Spoon batter into aebleskiver pan (each well should be full); turn when bubbles form on top.

Traditional Recipe

3 eggs, separated
2 Tablespoons sugar
2 cups buttermilk
2 cups flour
2 teaspoons baking powder
1 teaspoon baking soda
1 teaspoon salt

Mix sugar and buttermilk with egg yolks. Sift flour, baking soda, baking powder and salt. Add flour mixture to buttermilk mixture and mix until smooth. Beat egg whites until stiff and fold into buttermilk mixture. Spoon batter into aebleskiver pan (each well should be full); turn when bubbles form on top. Makes approximately 40.

JULIE ROHRER, CASTLE ROCK, COLORADO

JANSSON'S TEMPTATION

My maternal grandfather came to the USA at about age 20 from Sweden. As children, we enjoyed food from our heritage with him and my maternal Finnish grandmother. This is usually served at Christmas and Easter or as a late night snack. Excellent with Swedish meatballs. It's not too salty because Swedish anchovies are cured in a sweet brine and not very fishy.

You may also prepare it with a can of salmon and milk, instead of Swedish flat anchovies and heavy cream. That's the way my mom always prepared it. We called it Lox Lota. You may also use peeled, sliced celery root in place of half the potatoes.

4-5 medium potatoes, roughly grated
1 small can of Swedish flat anchovies (about 4 ounces)
1 large onion, thingly sliced
salt and pepper
1 1/4 cups of heavy cream

Preheat oven to 425°. Mix the potatoes with the onions, and add a little bit of salt and pepper. Put half of the mix in a buttered oven proof dish. Top with all of the anchovies. Add the rest of the potatoes and onions. Drizzle half of the cream on top, and put it in the oven. After 20 minutes, add the rest of the cream. Bake until it has some color – about 20 minutes more – so 40 minutes total.

MICHELLE ALSTER, COMSTOCK PARK, MICHIGAN

Russia and Eastern Europe

The mainstays of Eastern European cuisine were founded on the ingredients of peasant cuisine, prior to the 18th century. Local food sources provided ample fish, game, mushrooms, root vegetables, berries and grains and from these came a variety of soups and baked goods that remain staples of the cuisine.

Russia's court cuisine, at its peak, rivaled that of France and China in terms of skill and extravagance. Emperors and other wealthy families at the time imported chefs from France and elsewhere in western Europe, creating a new Franco-Russian cuisine which featured extravagant displays of complex and sophisticated dishes. Indeed, the famous French chef Marie-Antoine Carême served as chef to Tsar Alexander at the beginning of the 19th century, before returning to Paris. Carême created one of the more famous dishes to come out of this era, Charlotte Russe (*Russe* is French for Russian). Other well-known dishes that are products of Franco-Russian chefs are Beef Stroganoff and Chicken Kiev.

Another export of Russian court cuisine that has lasted to modern day is the concept of Russian service, brought back to France. This practice of having servers deliver individual dishes to the table, and directly serving the guests, provides for speedy service and visual spectacle.

Here in Calgary we do not lack for Eastern European delights, since western Canada has a strong Ukrainian community. My son's preschool is next door to a Slavic food store, and the aromas are irresistible: every afternoon a good portion of the moms can be found snacking on pierogi and blini when they came to pick up their kids.

BORSCHT

In Russia, it's borscht, in Poland, it's barszcz, and in northern China, which traded with Russia, it's known simply as "red soup." This hearty soup has umpteen variations, depending on who is cooking it. Generally speaking, it is served either hot or cold, and usually (but not always) includes beets. When I was growing up the taste of borscht was akin to punishment, when every kid had to "at least try it." Years later, when dining with my sisters at the Little Russian Café in Boulder, Colorado, we ordered it, and wincing, I tried it, shocked to discover how delicious it can be. Inspired by that evening, I will include the Russian variation here.

3 cups water
3 cups vegetable stock
1/2 tablespoon Kosher salt
1/2 cup finely chopped carrots
1/2 stalk celery, chopped
2 medium beets, cut into 1/2 inch slices
3 Russet potatoes, cut into 1 inch slices
5 Tablespoons butter, divided
1/2 cup chopped onion
2 cups canned tomatoes
3 cups finely shredded cabbage, divided
1 tablespoon dried dill weed

1/4 cup heavy cream
3/4 cup diced potatoes
salt and freshly ground black pepper to taste
1/2 cup sour cream
1 Tablespoon finely chopped fresh dill

Place water, stock, salt, carrots, celery, beets, and potato slices in a large stock-pot over high heat. Bring to a boil.

Melt 4 Tablespoons of butter in a separate skillet over medium heat. Sauté onions in butter until tender, approximately 5 minutes. Stir in 2 cups of cab-bage, sauté two minutes more, then add tomatoes and dill weed and reduce heat to medium low, and simmer for 15 minutes. Remove beets and potatoes with a slotted spoon or tongs, and place in a bowl with remaining 1 table-spoon of butter and the cream. Mash together until smooth.

Add diced potatoes to stock and simmer until just tender but still firm, ap-proximately 5 minutes. Increase heat to a low boil, and stir in remaining cab-bage, tomato sauce, and mashed beets and potatoes. Reduce heat and simmer a few minutes more. Season with salt and black pepper, garnish with sour cream and fresh dill, and serve.

BEEF STROGANOFF

Beef Stroganoff has traveled far and wide in its popularity. It is served in Iran, South Africa, Australia, and of course Europe and North America. Stroganoff has also migrated to Brazil and Portugal, where it is called estroganofe. In Brazil it is so popular, there is a chain of fast-food restaurants dedicated to it, called Stroganophy's.

Because of the sour cream, some stroganoff recipes can take on a rather unap-petizing gray color. I'm sorry, but who wants to eat anything gray? This recipe accentuates the beef flavor with the use of caramelized tomato paste, beef stock and red wine. The end result is a stroganoff with a nice, deep brown finish.

3 Tablespoons butter
1 pound sirloin steak, cut into thin strips
4 cups sliced mushrooms
1 onion, sliced thinly
2 Tablespoons tomato paste
1 teaspoon flour
1/2 cup red wine
1 cup beef stock or broth
2/3 cup sour cream
salt and pepper to taste
2 Tablespoons minced fresh parsley
12 ounces egg noodles

Start a big pot of water on high heat to cook egg noodles. Melt one Tablespoon of butter in large sauté pan. Add sirloin strips, working in batches if necessary to achieve a nice browning (versus crowding the pan). Set aside and keep warm, covered on a plate. Add remaining butter to the same pan, and sauté mushrooms and onions over medium-high heat. When they have softened, add tomato paste and continue cooking until all three are nicely caramelized. While they are cooking, add those egg noodles to your boiling water and cook according to package directions.

Add flour to onion and mushroom mixture and stir together for about one minute. Add wine and beef stock, scraping up any browned bits from the bottom of the pan. Bring to a gentle boil, and continue cooking for 5-10 minutes at a low boil to thicken the sauce. Reduce heat and add sour cream. Cook until sour cream has warmed through, and season to taste with salt and pepper. Serve over hot egg noodles and garnish with parsley.

PIEROGI, BLINI AND BLINTZES

Different types of pierogi appear throughout Europe and North America, each with their own spelling, and variations of filled, steamed dumplings are found throughout Asia as well. Here in Alberta, home to many of Ukrainian descent, we can proudly boast of being the home of the world's largest pierogi, a 25-foot fiberglass gem found in the town of Glendon (we also have the world's largest Ukrainian Easter egg, or pysanka, in Vegreville). In the Ukraine pierogi are also called varenyky.

Blini on the other hand are essentially thin pancakes, either filled or served flat with toppings, and come in many varieties both sweet and savory. The word comes from the Old Slavic *mlin*, or "to mill." Prior to the introduction of Christianity, they had religious significance: the pancakes were served at the end of winter to celebrate the coming spring in a festival called Maslenitsa (since they are round, they are shaped like the sun). Orthodox Christianity adopted the practice and it continues today, around the same time others are celebrating Mardi Gras or Shrove Tuesday. Blintzes became popular in the United States through Jewish immigrants, who brought the tradition with them.

BREAKFAST BLINI TORTE

This recipe is a bit of a "cheater" – it's not really blini, or blintzes, but it's a heck of a lot easier than making individual ones, and when you've got three kids, easy is good. For the fruit filling, I usually use "spoon fruit" from American Spoon, but any good-quality fruit preserves or thickened fruit sauce will do.

> 1 1/2 cups ricotta cheese
> 2 Tablespoons butter, softened
> 1 egg
> 1 Tablespoon sour cream
> 1/2 teaspoon salt

1 1/4 cups all-purpose flour
1 teaspoon baking powder
1/2 cup butter, softened
1/4 cup white sugar
2 eggs
3/4 cup milk
1 teaspoon vanilla

Preheat oven to 350° and lightly grease an 8" square baking dish.

Mix ricotta cheese, butter, egg, sour cream and salt in a small bowl. In a separate bowl, mix flour, baking powder, butter and sugar, then stir in eggs, milk and vanilla. Immediately place 1/2 the flour mixture in the baking dish. Cover with the cottage cheese mixture, then preserves, and top with remaining flour mixture.

Bake 50 minutes in the preheated oven, until puffed and golden brown. Allow torte to cool slightly, and cut into squares to serve. Garnish with a dollop of sour cream and fresh blueberries (or any fruit that pairs well with your preserves). Can also be served cold.

POLISH SAUSAGE & KRAUT

Editor's Note: West Michigan has a strong Polish community, which is celebrated during the Pulaski Days Festival in October, and the appearance every spring of the filled doughnuts known as paczki. My friend Renee, an excellent cook, married into a big Polish family and supplied this recipe. I must point out that when I had just had my second baby, Renee came over with supper for me, even though she was busy with four small kids of her own, including newborn twins. Now that's friendship!

Sauerkraut has been around for centuries, with different versions appearing in European, American and Asian cuisines. Sauerkraut served with sausage is a popular dish in Poland and Germany, and in France it is known as choucroute garnie – choucroute being the francophone pronunciation of sauerkraut.

Because the fermentation process preserves the vitamin C within the cabbage, sauerkraut was consumed on seafaring ships to avoid scurvy. When Captain James Cook forced his men to eat it, he did not lose one sailor to the disease. For making this connection and saving countless lives, the Royal Society of London awarded him the Copley Medal for achievement in science, an honor shared later by Albert Einstein, Stephen Hawking and Watson and Crick.

10 Polish sausages, cut into pieces (I cut each sausage into 4 pieces)
1 -2 Granny Smith apples, diced (no need to peel)
2 cans of sauerkraut - any brand is fine
1/4 cup of brown sugar (you can add more or less, depending upon how sweet you like the kraut)

Preheat oven to 325°. Put all ingredients into a casserole dish and cover; cook for 2-3 hours. The slower you cook, the more tender and juicy the Polish sausage is. I do take off the cover every 1/2 hour and stir, to keep the flavors mixing.

RENEE SCHAB, JENISON, MICHIGAN

POTATO CAKES WITH MUSHROOM SAUCE

This is my attempt to duplicate one of my favorite dishes from this great little restaurant in Boulder, Colorado. The Little Russian Cafe is no longer in business, but when Lionel and I were students there, we frequented this one quite often…. my sister Lisa can vouch for it, as well. Probably no more than 12 tables, deep red walls with fabulous paintings of zaftig Russian-looking women gracing the room. A separate menu for the various vodkas they had chilling in the freezer (to help aid in the digestion of this rich food) was much fun to sample from, and the chef and all of the staff were straight from the motherland. The Gypsy Mandolin was a duo who played folk music there on Friday and Saturdays, so cue up the CD player, peel some potatoes, and lets get cooking! PROST!

1 pound russet potatoes, cubed with skin left on
2 Tablespoons butter
2 egg whites
1/2 cup flour

Cook potatoes, drain. Add butter, and mash. Add salt and pepper to taste. Mix in egg whites and form into 6 balls. Flatten balls and coat in flour. Spray nonstick skillet, and fry until golden brown and warmed through.

Sauce:
6 ounces sliced mushrooms
1 cup chopped onion
1 1/2 cup vegetable stock
1 Tablespoon flour

Sauté mushrooms and onion in olive oil over medium heat. Stir in flour, and cook 1 minute. Add vegetable stock all at once and stir; heat until thickened. Season to taste with salt and pepper. Pour over potato cakes. Serves 4 as a side dish or 2 as a main dish.

CINDY LOZA, MARION, IOWA

YUGOSLAVIAN NUT HORNS

My mom (who was half Yugoslavian) always made these ahead for Christmas then put them in tins and hid them from my Dad (he still found them) until Christmas!

Dough:
4 cups flour
1/2 teaspoon salt
1 envelope dry yeast
1 cup sour cream
3 egg yolks (reserve whites)
1 1/4 cup butter, chilled and cut into small pieces

Filling:
Reserved egg whites
1 cup sugar
1 cup finely chopped walnuts
1/2 teaspoon vanilla

Mix flour, yeast and salt in a large bowl. Add butter and cut in with a pastry blender, until it resembles small peas. Mix egg yolks and sour cream in a small bowl. Add in flour mixture and stir until it forms a ball.

In a small, deep bowl beat egg white on high until soft peaks form. Beat in sugar 1/4 cup at a time until thick and glossy. Fold in nuts and vanilla. Preheat oven to 350°. Cut dough into 8 equal pieces. Sprinkle 1 Tablespoon of sugar on work surface and roll out one piece of dough into a 9" circle. Spread with 3 Tablespoons filling and cut into 8 wedges. Starting at the wide end of each wedge, roll up tightly. Roll each horn in sugar, form a curve and place 1" apart on an ungreased cookie sheet. Repeat with remaining pieces of dough. Bake at 350° for 20 minutes, or until lightly browned. Remove, cool and store in an airtight container. These are better when they sit at least a couple of days to a week.

TERI MERCIER, CALGARY, ALBERTA

Spain and
the Basque Region

Spain's cuisine today is the descendant of Roman, North African, Middle Eastern and Greek cuisines, mixed with the ingredients and traditions of the New World. Like other countries in Europe, there are distinct regions with unique dialects and cuisines, but in all cases fish and seafood are central to the diet.

Contrary to many assumptions, it is Spain, not Italy or Greece, that is the world's largest producer – and consumer – of olive oil. During the heydays of the Roman Empire, Spain shipped countless numbers of amphorae (slender clay vessels made for shipping), filled with olive oil, to Rome. According to Sarah Murray's recent book *Moveable Feasts*, historians and archaeologists estimate that over 1.6 billion amphorae of olive oil were moved from Spain to Rome for the benefit of the empire: in terms of volume, this is the equivalent of flushing a toilet once per second – for *32 years*.

Olive trees are cousins of jasmine and lilac, which is explains the fragrance of its fruit and wood. Mediterranean olives like those found in Spain contain more oleocanthal than California varieties, the chemical compound that makes the stuff so healthy in the first place (this is not to disparage California olives, which are still pretty darn healthy).

Spain also enjoys extensive groves of almond and orange trees, brought from North Africa and cultivated to a greater extent by the Moors during their occupation, but it is bread, olive oil, and wine that are essential to Spanish cuisine overall.

Regional differences in cuisine mark the patterns of human movement through Spain's history. The Basque people have been in northern Spain for centuries. The northern region that lies along the Atlantic is Galicia: the same tribes that made it into Ireland, Scotland and Wales also landed here, and you'll find bagpipes, Irish whiskey and tales of leprechauns. The central body of Spain, running north to south, features Moor-introduced spices used more liberally in the south (cumin and cinnamon), and tapas more popular in the middle.

If you want to throw a Spanish dinner party, you could feature a sampling of regional cuisine through tapas, including the popular dish of chickpeas with spinach, or a simple mixed salad with paella. On a hot evening you could also offer a cool bowl of gazpacho to start things off and in doing so indulge your guests with some trivia: gazpacho is yet another feature of Spanish cuisine adopted from the Moors, and originally it did not include tomatoes (they would come later, across the Atlantic).

The Basque
With over 5,000 years of history, the Basque people are identified as the oldest ethnic group in Europe. They are not directly related to Indo-Europeans, and their language is not connected to any other European language (the Basque term is *Euskaldunak*, or Basque-speaker). Straddling the line between France and Spain, and separated from one another by steep mountains and coastlines,

they have many regional differences and yet continue to hold fiercely to their identity, and in Spain some Basque regions actually possess a limited amount of autonomy. To put it in terms of popular culture, this is the region that includes the tony resorts of Biarritz, the storied pilgrim routes of Santiago de Compostela, the tragic history of Guernica portrayed by Picasso in his masterwork painting, the daring architecture of Frank Gehry's Guggenheim Museum in Bilbao, and the running of the bulls in Pamplona.

Basques have been excellent fishermen for centuries, and their cuisine benefits from almost every fish and seafood imaginable. Indeed, it is possible that centuries ago Basque fishermen, on the hunt for whales, may have traveled as far as the Grand Banks. The Basque region is coastal but also mountainous, and the other main foodstuff consequently comes from sheep that can negotiate the steep cliffs. Lamb and sheep's milk cheeses are common ingredients in Basque cooking, as are chilies, peppers and other fresh vegetables and herbs. Bayonne ham, salted and unsmoked, is well-known for its quality and appears in many Basque dishes. Many ingredients used in Basque cooking can be found easily in North America, but Bayonne ham is not one of them. A good quality prosciutto can be used instead. Ironically, two of the most prominent Basque ingredients, chestnuts and cherries, can be found just down the road at my cousin's farm, DeKleine Orchards in Hudsonville, Michigan. In the summer, stop by to get your fill!

Basque people love to eat: indeed, an old Basque saying claims, "if you know how to eat, you know enough." Meals are either a family affair, set at large tables with plenty of food, often beginning with a soup course, or as part of the male-dominated dining clubs that are popular in this region. Men often do the cooking, so if you are hosting a Basque-style dinner party, well guys, it's time to step up!

GAZPACHO

Editor's Note: Believe it or not, the recipe for gazpacho originally did not include tomatoes. It originated in the southern Spanish region of Andalusia, and its foundations were stale bread, garlic, olive oil, salt and vinegar, likely influenced by the Moors' culinary imports.

To quickly peel tomatoes, slice a small "X" in the top of each and blanch for a few seconds in boiling water. Remove and cool. Peeling will be much easier.

- 1 cup finely chopped peeled tomatoes
- 1/2 cup each finely chopped yellow or orange pepper, celery and cucumber
- 1/4 cup finely chopped onion
- 2 teaspoons snipped parsley
- 1 teaspoon snipped chives
- 1 clove garlic, minced
- 2-3 Tablespoons tarragon wine vinegar
- 2 Tablespoons olive oil
- 1/2 teaspoon Worcestershire sauce
- 1 teaspoon salt
- 1/4 teaspoon ground black pepper
- 2 cups tomato juice

Combine all ingredients in stainless steel or glass bowl. Cover and chill at least 4 hours. Serve in chilled mugs or bowls with croutons.

SANDRA ANDERSON, TUCSON, ARIZONA

COQUILLES ST. JACQUES

This is actually a classic French dish, but its origin comes from the story of St. Jacques, known as Saint James in English and as Sant' Iago in Spain. Hundreds of years ago, ardent Christians traveled the pilgrim route across the Basque region and through Northern Spain to reach Santiago de Compostela, the church that contained the saint's remains. In one of the stories associated with St. Jacques, he rescues a groomsman from the sea and as said groomsman emerges from the water, he is draped with cockleshells around his shoulders. From this legend we have the French invention of Coquilles St. Jacques.

1 cup water
1 cup white wine
16 ounces bay scallops
1 bay leaf
dash cayenne powder
4 Tablespoons butter
1/4 cup chopped fresh parsley
1 onion, minced
4 Tablespoons flour
1 clove garlic, minced
2 egg yolks, beaten
1/3 cup heavy whipping cream
1 cup chopped mushrooms (I use Porcini)
1/2 cup bread crumbs
1/2 cup freshly grated Parmesan

In a skillet combine first six ingredients. Simmer scallops no more than 5 minutes or until cooked. Drain, reserving cooking liquid. In same skillet melt butter and sauté onion until tender: add flour and garlic, and sauté about one minute more. Stir in reserved liquid and cook, reducing until sauce has thickened.

Temper eggs yolks with a little bit of sauce, then add yolks and stir in quickly. Add scallops and mushrooms, heat gently and pour into eight ramekins or small bowls. Mix breadcrumbs and Parmesan together and sprinkle on top. Place ramekins on a cookie sheet and bake at 425° until golden brown – about 5 minutes.

GATEAU BASQUE

Gateau Basque is a well-known dessert in the Basque region of southern France and northern Spain. These cakes usually have a pastry cream or cherry and cream filling, often distinguished by the appearance of a Basque cross on the cherry version. The "cake" part of this treat is closer to a tart dough and is rolled out just like pastry, but the addition of baking powder means it will puff up like a cake in the oven.

Those familiar with French pastry making will likely be mortified by the low-brow substitution of instant pudding for homemade pastry cream. If you find yourself in this category, by all means accept my apologies and insert your favorite pastry cream recipe here. But I will tell you that this version is infinitely easier, and hey, you get to eat your cake that much faster.

If you don't have a springform pan, any small cake pan or round casserole dish will do: your servings might not cut as neatly, but it will taste just as good.

Pastry:
1 stick (1/2 cup) unsalted butter, at room temperature
1/2 cup sugar
1/8 teaspoon salt
1 egg
1 egg yolk
1 teaspoon almond paste
1 1/2 cups all-purpose flour
1 teaspoon baking powder

Filling:

1 3.4 ounce (4-serving) package French vanilla instant pudding

1 1/2 cups cold milk

1 1/2 cups nondairy whipped topping

3/4 cup sour cherry preserves (I use American Spoon Sour Cherry Spoon Fruit)

1 egg and 1 Tablespoon milk, beaten and set aside, for egg wash

To make the pastry, cream butter, sugar and salt together until fluffy, using an electric mixer on low speed. Add the egg and egg yolk and mix until blended. In a small bowl, blend flour and baking powder. Add the flour mixture to the butter mixture and mix on low speed until a soft dough forms. Divide dough into two pieces, wrap each in plastic wrap, and chill in refrigerator until firm, at least 30 minutes.

Make pudding according to directions. Gently fold in whipped topping. Place a sheet of plastic wrap on surface of pudding mixture to prevent a skin from forming, and chill until ready to use.

Preheat oven to 325°. Set prepared cake pan on a baking sheet lined with aluminum foil. Working between two sheets of plastic wrap, roll or press each piece of dough to a 9-inch round. Remove wrap and place one piece in the bottom of the pan, pressing it into the corners and up the sides. Spread preserves evenly over bottom pastry layer, and then add pudding mixture, spreading carefully over preserves. Place second piece of rolled dough on top of pudding mixture, and press edges of dough together as much as possible. Using a sharp knife, lightly score the top layer of dough in a criss-cross pattern, then brush cake with egg wash. With the tip of the knife, poke three holes in the top to allow steam to escape.

Bake one hour or until top is golden brown. Transfer cake to a wire rack and allow it to cool completely. Serve room temperature or chilled.

NORTH AMERICA, CENTRAL AMERICA AND THE CARIBBEAN

Canada

When in comes to Canadian history, I must admit like many of my fellow Americans I am pretty ignorant. So it was with great relish that I discovered – or in some cases remembered – some fascinating highlights – pertaining to food, of course. Following the progression of European settlement, like America, we shall move East to West. Here goes:

While First Nations peoples likely came to Canada from Asia across the land bridge of the Bering Strait and *remained*, the Vikings of Scandinavia that landed on the eastern shore made their mark, stayed for a while, and then went home never to return, years before Columbus set sail.

Later, the Atlantic region off the southeast coast of Newfoundland known today as the Grand Banks, altered the face of cuisine across the world by means of its abundant resources. This part of the Atlantic, teeming with cod and other fish and marine mammals, was most likely discovered separately by Vikings, Basque fishermen on wayward whaling expeditions, and finally "officially" by English sailor John Cabot in 1497.

For centuries, cod was fished in the Grand Banks, then salted on board and transported to Europe, Africa, and North America, and was used to feed slaves on the plantations of the Caribbean. This salt cod once served simply as an economical food source, but is now revered worldwide. Indeed, ackee and saltfish is the national dish of Jamaica: the Portuguese version, bacalao, is popular in Europe and South America, and saltfish is popular in south India as well. Years ago, in exchange for saltfish, Jamaica supplied Newfoundland with rum and today Newfoundland "screech" rum continues to be a popular regional liquor. According to legend, the rum gets its name from the sound made by a visiting American soldier when he took a swig. Strong stuff:

"This delightful product may have continued indefinitely as a nameless rum except for the influx of American servicemen to Newfoundland during World War II.

As the story goes, the commanding officer of the first detachment was taking advantage of Newfoundland hospitality for the first time and was offered a drop of rum as an after dinner drink. Seeing his host toss back the liquor with nary a quiver, the unsuspecting American adhered to local custom and downed the drink in one gulp.

The look of shock and the glorious shades of color on the American's face were overshadowed by the bloodcurdling howl made by the poor fellow as he managed to regain his breath. Sympathetic persons from miles around rushed to the house to assist the poor man in such obvious agony and of course to satisfy their curiosity as to what was going on. Among the first to arrive was a garrulous old American sergeant who pounded on the door and demanded "What the cripes was that ungodly screech?"

The taciturn Newf who had answered the door replied simply, "The screech?" 'Tis the rum, me son."

-Newfoundland Labrador Liquor Corporation

I love that story. But I digress – back to our micro-history lesson:

The next major phase of Canadian culinary history is tied primarily to the move westward, either through the enticement of farming large expanses of grain on the prairies, or through the expansion of the railroad, or through the vast, open ranchlands of southern Alberta. Dried meat mixed with fat and dried berries, called pemmican, became a staple for those traveling through the middle regions of Canada, since food sources were not always reliable.

Today Canadian chefs proudly use local, organic ingredients (yes, that includes maple syrup) to highlight the riches of regional Canadian cuisine. Large immigrant populations, particularly from Asia, Europe and South America, have expanded the choices available to Canadian diners. In British Columbia, fish and seafood play a starring role in regional fare. Since much of the province is quite temperate, it actually enjoys a long growing season and "BC" cherries, peaches, and strawberries are particularly good. Additionally, a long strip down the center of the province known simply as "The Okanagan" is quickly becoming the hottest destination for food and wine lovers. Vineyards, orchards, beaches, marinas, and resorts dot the rolling hills surrounding Lake Okanagan. Famous Canadians like Jason Priestley are lending star power by purchasing interests in vineyards, and many of the locally produced wines are holding their own in international competition.

Calgary, Alberta
In terms of food and food culture, Calgary has a lot to be proud of. First of all, it is a very young city, so it hasn't had the time to develop a cuisine the way say, Rome or Paris, or even San Francisco has. But in the course of its short history it has created a vibrant culture: Bernard Callebaut, originally from Belgium, is

based in Calgary but is known worldwide for his high quality chocolate. Slow Food Calgary is a popular organization that recently helped to bring Barbara Kingsolver and Steven Hopp to the city to discuss their book *Animal, Vegetable, Miracle*. The Calgary Farmers' Market is open every weekend *year round* – that's saying something for a city that reaches –35° C. in the winter. And it is simply impossible to go hungry at the Calgary Stampede.

The Calgary Stampede (or simply "Stampede" as the locals call it) is to Calgary as Mardi Gras is to New Orleans, as the Kentucky Derby is to Louisville. For ten days in July, a celebration of Alberta's cowboy heritage takes over every part of the city. Oil and gas executives take a break from negotiations to sidle through downtown, donning cowboy hats and boots as they move from pancake breakfasts in the morning, to barbeques for lunch and dinner.

At the heart of Stampede is the Stampede Grounds, where the rodeo takes place: but to say the Calgary Stampede is a rodeo is like saying Mardi Gras is a parade and the Kentucky Derby is a horse race. The legendary Chuckwagon races, known locally as "the chucks," take place every evening after the rodeo, with heart-pounding, thunderous action as teams of horses and outriders whip around the racetrack competing for the big prize. Big-name concerts, a carnival, agricultural expo, First Nations village, a casino, entertainment, and endless food booths and vendors are also part of the action.

All across the city, celebrations take place including Stampede "caravan" parties that draw thousands each, offering free pancake breakfasts, entertainment and interactions with local celebrities. In addition, private businesses and organizations host free pancake breakfasts and barbeques: play your cards right, and you can eat free for two weeks in July. During these same weeks, neighbors and friends often get together, combine their barbeques and have hoedowns of their own. In the spirit of these Stampede block parties, I offer a collection of recipes inspired by cowboy culture from around the world (to sample Boulder Stew, see the Western States section).

Cowboys: A Culinary History

The biggest cattle boom in Canadian history occurred in Alberta during the last decades of the 19th century. As a way to celebrate Alberta's cowboy heritage, local man Guy Weadick created the Calgary Exhibition and Stampede in 1912. In recent years Calgary's "cowtown" image has been modernized by the influx of oil and gas companies, taking advantage of the oil sands in northern Alberta. Even so, cattle remains an important part of the economy, and Alberta beef is widely recognized as being of particularly high quality.

Western Canada shares its strong horsemanship traditions with many other cultures, of course. In the same way certain cooking traditions fanned across the globe, so too horse breeding began with Arab cultures, and spread through Spain when the Moors arrived from North Africa in the 8th century. Several hundred years later, Spanish conquistadors brought horses and the practice of breeding to the Americas. The rapid spread of Spanish influence gave rise to cowboy traditions from South to North America. In Chile, for example, it is the *huaso* who must negotiate monsoon-like conditions when driving cattle. *Vaquieros* in the northern part of Brazil herd cattle on dry plains, and Argentina and Uruguay are home to the *gaucho*, who rides the grassy plains, or *pampas*. Prior to the establishment of ranches by wealthy landowners, these gauchos primarily hunted wild cattle instead of herding. In Mexico, *vaqueros* were working cowboys, whereas the *chollos* were landed gentry who practiced equestrian skills.

Horsemanship and cattle ranching spread beyond the Americas to Hawaii when Captain George Vancouver, for whom the city in British Columbia is named, presented King Kamehameha with five head of cattle as a gift. The cattle quickly reproduced and took over, and soon the King needed assistance to manage the growing herd. Spanish cowboys from Mexico and California were brought in and the paniolo culture was born (*paniolo* was adapted from the Spanish *espagnol*, or Spaniard).

In mainland United States, of course, the image of the American cowboy is iconic. Put on the country music, strike up the grill and cowboy up!

NEW WORLD POLENTA

Maple syrup from Canada, chipotle chiles from Mexico and corn and sweet potatoes from across the Americas combine to create a sweet and spicy dish. To save time, you can make it the night before and then bake it right before serving.

One cardboard container of vegetable broth plus enough water to make 5 1/2 cups
1 chipotle pepper in adobo, seeded and minced
1 teaspoon kosher salt
2 large sweet potatoes or yams, peeled and cut in one-inch dice
3/4 cup chopped onion
1/2 teaspoon fresh rosemary, chopped fine
1 Tablespoon olive oil
1 3/4 cups cornmeal
1/2 cup maple syrup
2 cups fresh or frozen corn kernels
salt and pepper to taste

Bring the stock, water, chile, salt and sweet potatoes to a boil. Simmer until potatoes are tender. Remove potatoes with a slotted spoon, and mash in a bowl with 2 cups of the cooking liquid. Reserve remaining liquid. Sauté onion and rosemary in olive oil 2 minutes, and add cooking liquid and sweet potato mixture. Bring to a boil and slowly whisk in cornmeal. Reduce heat and cook for 20 minutes, stirring constantly.

Remove from heat, add corn and maple syrup and season to taste with salt and pepper. Pour into lightly oiled 9 x 13 pan; cover and refrigerate for at least one hour (or up to a day), until firm. Heat oven to 350°. Cut polenta into squares or triangles and place on a lightly greased baking sheet. Bake for 15 minutes.

SWISS CHARD POLENTA

This was Adam's first request when I brought up the idea of doing a cookbook, so it simply had to be included. You may be wondering why it's here instead of in the Italy section, but like the other polenta recipe, it goes exceptionally well with ribeye steaks and a tossed salad. Try them both and decide what you like best. We get rainbow chard from the Calgary Farmer's Market and it's just beautiful – sometimes I buy double and use the rest as a centerpiece!

> 2 bunches Swiss chard (I use the "rainbow" variety for color)
> 1 Tablespoon olive oil
> 4 cloves garlic, minced
> 1/2 cup finely chopped onion
> 1 3/4 cup water
> 1 15-ounce can chicken broth
> 1 cup polenta or cornmeal
> 1 cup shredded mozzarella cheese
> 3 Tablespoons freshly grated Parmesan cheese
> 1/4 cup sour cream or ricotta cheese

Remove stems and thickest part of ribs from chard. Clean leaves thoroughly, then chop ribs and leaves coarsely (do not dry chard after cleaning). Heat oil in large skillet or shallow pan, and add onion and garlic. Sauté for one minute, then add chard. Cover and cook 4-6 minutes, stirring once or twice. Set aside.

Heat water and broth in saucepan. Slowly pour in polenta, stirring quickly with a whisk. Bring mixture to a boil, then reduce heat and cook until stock is absorbed and polenta is cooked, about 7-10 minutes. Stir in mozzarella and Parmesan cheeses.

Preheat oven to 375°. Pour half of polenta into a lightly greased casserole dish. Top with chard mixture, then dollop sour cream or ricotta on top of chard. Add remaining polenta and spread evenly to edges of casserole. Bake for 20-30 minutes, or until polenta is golden brown and bubbly. Allow to rest slightly before serving.

BARBEQUED ALBERTA BEEF RIBEYE STEAKS

Although we associate barbeque with western or southwestern cuisine, the word actually originates from the Caribbean. Arawak Indians, the first inhabitants of the Caribbean islands, cooked their meat on a *brabacot*, a wooden framework set over coals. The Spanish later converted this to *barbacoa* and brought it with them into Mexico and Florida. The rest, as they say, is history.

If you can't get Alberta beef, well, first my deepest sympathy. Secondly, any other beef will do just fine. Allowing the steaks to rest at room temperature will make for a more tender end result.

    4 Ribeye steaks
    1/4 cup olive oil
    1/4 cup Montreal steak seasoning

Rub olive oil on steaks, then rub in steak seasoning. Allow steaks to rest at room temperature for 15 minutes prior to grilling. Heat grill to medium, and grill steaks to desired doneness. Serves 4.

BEET AND GOAT CHEESE SALAD

Okay, clearly this is not cowboy fare: but this salad goes really well with the rib-eye steak recipe above. These two, along with the Swiss Chard Polenta and/or the New World Polenta is what we serve our out-of-town guests, so they can sample Alberta beef and the treasures from the local farmers' market. The salad recipe was originally inspired by a trip with my husband to River Café, a fabulous restaurant situated on an island on the Bow River, in downtown Calgary. I had a salad with similar ingredients shortly after moving to Canada, and after having a baby, selling the house and moving, it was my first "grown-up" meal in months – it was so good, I almost cried!

2-4 beets, depending on size
1 bag of baby spinach, baby romaine or field greens salad
1/2 cup balsamic vinaigrette
1 log goat cheese
1 cup walnuts
1/2 cup maple syrup

Preheat oven to 400°. Scrub beet skins, prick, and roast in oven until fork-tender. Allow beets to cool, then peel and cut in large chunks. Set aside. Toss salad greens with vinaigrette in serving bowl, and allow to chill in refrigerator while preparing remaining ingredients. Toast walnuts gently in a dry sauté pan, just until you sense their aroma. Stir in maple syrup and remove from heat.

When you are ready to assemble the salad, toss greens once more, then add beets on top. Sprinkle goat cheese over top, and spoon glazed walnuts on top of the salad.

PULLED ALBERTA BEEF SANDWICHES

Alberta beef plays a prominent role in the annual Calgary Stampede, either as midway food, like these walking pulled beef sandwiches, or as prime rib roasts in some of the higher-end eating establishments on Stampede grounds.

1 Tablespoon vegetable oil
5-6 pounds of beef roast, well marbled
3 carrots, chopped in large chunks
1 large onion, quartered

2 bay leaves
4 large garlic cloves smashed
2 ribs celery, cut in large chunks
1 teaspoon Kosher salt
1 teaspoon thyme
1 teaspoon cumin
1 teaspoon ancho chili powder
1 12 ounce bottle of good quality beer
1 large bottle of your favorite barbeque sauce

Heat oil in a large pot and brown roast quickly on all sides. Add all ingredients except the barbeque sauce, and cover with water. Bring to a boil, then cover and gently simmer for 2 - 2 1/2 hours, or until meat can be pulled apart easily. Remove meat from pot and allow to rest for 5-10 minutes, reserving liquid. In a large bowl or on a large cutting board, shred the beef with 2 forks. Add barbeque sauce and one cup cooking liquid. Serve on toasted hamburger buns.

BISON BURGERS

Our family has stopped eating ground beef altogether, and we now purchase only ground bison. We are lucky to have a few good choices readily available to us here in Calgary. Bison meat has less fat and cholesterol than chicken, and the taste, in my humble opinion, is superior to that of beef. Because it is so lean it makes cooking somewhat tricky, but ground bison is moist enough that you don't need to worry about the meat drying out.

1 1/2 pounds ground bison
Montreal steak seasoning
5 hamburger buns

Preheat grill. Form patties from ground bison and put on a platter. Sprinkle steak seasoning on one side, press into patties. Flip patties over and repeat on the other side. Grill to desired doneness. Toast buns and serve. Makes 5 burgers.

The Caribbean

The history and culture of the Caribbean conjures romantic and storied images: pirates with names like Henry Morgan and Blackbeard, the musical and political force of Bob Marley, and the visual treasure it is to behold mountainous green islands shooting up from bright turquoise waters. To describe the incredible diversity of cultures and cuisines present in the Caribbean would be a very large book in itself. While there are as many different approaches to food as there are islands, there are a few common threads that run through this tropical paradise.

First, almost all Caribbean cuisines owe their identity at least in part to Africa. African slaves were brought to the region by the thousands from the 1500s to the early 1800s. They brought with them new ingredients, including watermelon and okra, and methods of cooking which carry over to today. To a lesser extent, East Indian and Chinese populations also impacted the region following the abolition of slavery, when Indian and Chinese laborers were brought in as indentured servants to work the land.

Caribbean cuisine is also influenced by the countries that, at one point, colonized certain islands: as a result, the previously Spanish-held islands of Cuba, Dominican Republic, and Puerto Rico have a strong Latin identity. Martinique, St. Martin, Haiti, and St. Bartolémy maintain strong French culture, and Sint Maarten and the "ABC" islands of Aruba, Bonaire and Curaçao still maintain a Dutch identity. Still other islands, including Jamaica, the Bahamas, Bermuda, St. Lucia and Trinidad and Tobago, carry cultural vestiges of their days as English colonies.

Finally, an emphasis on freshness is a commonality among islands, particularly in terms of fish, seafood, fruits and vegetables. The Caribbean is rich with a variety of readily available fish such as grouper, mahi mahi, snapper, conch, marlin, and more: the most common way to prepare it is with a minimal amount of fuss, provided the fish is exceptionally fresh. If you're lucky enough to visit Trinidad, don't leave without trying the cascadura: eating it is said to guarantee you a return trip.

Tropical produce, such as mango, pineapple, banana, soursop, chayote, watermelon, avocado, lime and papaya are all grown in the Caribbean, and local farmers rely heavily on tubers such as yam, potato and cassava. Pork, chicken and goat are the most common meat sources, since many islands have mountainous terrains that make cattle farming problematic.

Some Caribbean produce is not for the careless chef: cassava, which is used throughout the region, must be prepared correctly since the juices that are strained from this root vegetable prior to preparation are highly toxic. The pods of the ackee fruit of Jamaica, used in Jamaica's national dish of ackee and saltfish, are extremely poisonous until fully ripened: the fruit is so potentially toxic, its import was originally banned by the United States. Curiously enough, it was the ill-fated Captain Bligh, on the HMS Bounty, who first brought ackee to Jamaica from Africa.

If you find yourself lucky enough to host a Caribbean potluck, make sure to include Cuban, reggae and calypso music in the background. At the table, use color to your advantage, using the well-known red, green, gold and black of Jamaica, or just bright, tropical colors that evoke a seaside atmosphere. You can play around with the meal, but I would recommend some type of grilled meat or fish, combined with a rice and bean dish as a starting point.

MOROS Y CRISTIANOS (MOORS AND CHRISTIANS)

This is the ubiquitous dish of black beans (*moros*) and rice (the *cristianos* part of the equation), found throughout Cuba. There are many variations on it throughout the Caribbean and North America, likely because it provides a healthy, economic and quick-cooking meal. The title of the recipe recalls the time when the Moors invaded Spain and established cultural influences that would last for centuries.

3 Tablespoons olive oil
1 1/2 cups diced green and/or red peppers
2 cups diced onions
4 cloves of garlic, minced
1 1/2 teaspoons oregano
1 1/2 teaspoons cumin
1 teaspoon salt
1/2 teaspoon black pepper
3 cups drained canned black beans
1 small can of diced green chiles
1/2 cup fresh salsa
1 cup rice
2 cups chicken stock
1/4 cup chopped fresh cilantro

Heat olive oil in large saucepan. Sauté onions and peppers until tender, about four minutes. Add garlic, oregano, cumin, salt and pepper and sauté one minute more. Stir in black beans, chiles, salsa, rice and chicken stock. Bring to a boil, reduce heat, cover and simmer gently for 20 minutes or until rice is tender. Place in serving dish and garnish with cilantro. Makes 12 side-dish servings or 6 main-dish servings.

ROPA VIEJA WITH SOFRITO

Sofrito is a spicy, aromatic sauce used in many Caribbean dishes. Its name is connected to the Italian *soffritto* (sautéed) and actually applies to several different concoctions from many countries, including Cuba, Italy, Puerto Rico, the Greek island of Corfu and Sephardic cultures of the eastern Mediterranean. In each case the sauce – or dish – is something completely different. For our purposes here, it acts as a flavor base for the shredded beef.

Ropa Vieja also enjoys quite an international pedigree: it originally came from the Canary Islands, the last stop for mariners on their way from Spain to Cuba. Because of this historic link between the two island cultures, Cuban and Canarian cuisines – and even their dialects – are very similar. Ropa Vieja is Spanish for "old clothes" because the shredded beef looks like rags or torn clothes.

1/3 cup olive oil
3 pounds beef roast
1 carrot, cut in big chunks
2 celery ribs, cut in big chunks
1/2 onion, cut in big chunks
1 cup Rioja (Spanish red wine)
1 cup water
1 bay leaf
1 teaspoon cumin
2 cups Sofrito (see below)

Heat oil in large stockpot or pan. Place roast in pan and brown on all sides, on medium to high heat. Add vegetables, wine, water, bay leaf and cumin, reduce heat to low, cover and simmer for 1 1/2 to 2 hours, or until meat is cooked and tender. Move roast to a bowl or cutting board and reserve cooking liquid. Allow meat to rest for ten minutes, then shred with two forks.

Return shredded meat to pan, and add sofrito and one cup of reserved cooking liquid. Cook for 15 minutes, stirring occasionally.

Sofrito

Like pesto, sofrito can be made in advance and frozen in smaller portions to use as needed.

1 medium onion, diced
1 red pepper, diced
1 green pepper, diced
6 cloves of garlic, minced
1 teaspoon cumin
1/2 teaspoon salt
1/2 teaspoon pepper
2 medium tomatoes, diced

Sauté onions, tomatoes, garlic and peppers with cumin, salt and pepper until soft. Allow to cool slightly, then place in a blender or bowl of a food processor and blend briefly to make a thick, chunky sauce.

WEST INDIAN ROTIS WITH CHICKEN AND POTATO CURRY

Rotis are found throughout the Caribbean in many different forms, but are most prevalent on islands with large East Indian populations, such as Trinidad and Tobago. Roti refers to both the bread and the dish: rotis are a type of flatbread made on a large, flat pan over a fire or stove. In terms of fillings, again there are many types: they are almost always savory, and wrapped burrito-style in the roti. One exception is "buss-up-shut" (bursted up shirt), named for the way the dish appears – the roti bread is torn in shreds and served with the filling.

I was lucky enough to have my friend Vinita over for dinner when I attempted my first roti. She took one look at me, and one look at the pan and said, "can I help with anything?" Thank goodness she took over at the stove. The rotis were warm, buttery and pliable and a great complement to the curry. If you're in a pinch, large flour tortillas will do but the taste will be completely different.

2 1/2 cups all purpose flour
2 teaspoons baking powder
1 tablespoon butter, room temperature
3/4 cup of water
1 cup oil (melted butter can be used in place of oil during cooking process for a richer roti – make sure it doesn't smoke!)

2 pounds chicken thighs, cut into bite-sized pieces
2 tablespoons vegetable oil
1 large onion, chopped
3 garlic cloves, minced
1 inch piece of fresh ginger, minced
1 chili pepper (I use jalapeño), seeded and minced
4-5 medium potatoes, diced
2 tablespoons curry powder
1 teaspoon chili powder

1 teaspoon paprika
1 cup water or chicken stock
1/2 cup coconut milk
salt and pepper to taste

Filling:

Heat oil in large sauté pan. Add onions and sauté for two minutes; then add garlic, ginger, chili pepper and potato and continue cooking until fork-tender. Add spices and stir, then add chicken pieces: fry on medium heat for 10 minutes. Add water or stock and coconut milk; bring to a boil, then simmer, covered, for about 20 minutes or until chicken is tender. Keep warm on stove while you prepare the rotis.

Roti:

Sift flour, then add baking powder and butter. Mix well with fingers or with pastry cutter. Add water and knead to make a soft dough. Cut into 6 pieces. Roll each piece of dough out to a thin circle on a floured board. Apply oil to the surface, then sprinkle lightly with flour. Fold in half, then quarter, then roll into a ball. Let the dough pieces rest for 10 minutes. Roll out each piece thinly again, and place on a hot griddle or large sauté pan. Brush each side of dough with oil or butter to prevent sticking, turning frequently. Remove roti and slap back and forth with both hands until pliable. Place between sheets of waxed paper and serve hot.

MOJITOS

This recipe comes from my friend Michelle, who knows her way around a kitchen – and a cocktail shaker, for that matter. These are a refreshing treat to serve before a Caribbean theme dinner party on those sweltering summer days.

3 fresh mint sprigs
2 teaspoons sugar
3 Tablespoons fresh lime juice
1 1/2 ounces light rum
chilled club soda

In a tall thin glass, crush part of the mint with a fork to coat the inside. Add the sugar and lime juice and stir thoroughly. Top with ice. Add rum and mix. Top off with chilled club soda (or seltzer). Add a lime slice and the remaining mint, and serve.

MICHELLE ALSTER, COMSTOCK PARK, MICHIGAN

FRUITY MOJITOS

4 mint leaves
1-2 tsp sugar (to taste)
juice of 1/2 small lime
fresh fruit, as desired (raspberries, mango, blueberries, etc.)
1-1/2 to 2 oz rum or flavored rum
club soda

In a large glass, muddle these ingredients with a fork or blunt end of wooden spoon until mint leaves are bruised. Add ice as desired. Add rum and fill glass with club soda.

Stir and garnish with additional mint leaves, if desired.

STEVE GILLICH, GRAND RAPIDS, MICHIGAN

JAMAICAN JERK PORK

Jamaican jerk is a mixture of spices and seasonings that adds a kick to meats and fish. It was developed by the Maroons, a group of slaves in Jamaica who successfully rebelled against the plantation owners and acquired a limited amount of freedom: they were considered free people, but they had to stay within a small, mountainous region of the island. Perhaps for this reason, jerk remained almost totally unknown until the 1950s even though it was a fixture of Maroon cuisine. Since the spices were applied to meat that was then smoked, in order to preserve the meat, conventional wisdom holds that the word *jerk* came from *jerky*, which came from the Spanish word for dried meat, *charqui*.

Today jerk is commonly seen in Caribbean and North American restaurants, with varying degrees of heat. Many spice combinations are used throughout the Caribbean, but what makes jerk "jerk" is the intense scotch bonnet pepper and the addition of allspice. If you can't find scotch bonnets in your neighborhood, habañeros can be substituted. Keep in mind that if you do use Scotch bonnet peppers, these are some of the hottest in the world and plan accordingly! Use gloves when handling them, avoid touching your eyes, and wash everything in hot soapy water when you're done.

In Jamaica jerked meat and fish is often served with a type of fried cornbread called *festival*. Cornbread or corn muffins make a good substitute, because they can absorb the heat better than drinking water if the burn gets to be too much!

> 6-8 pounds boneless pork rib roast
> 1-4 sliced scotch bonnet peppers – (or 2-4 jalepeños for milder flavor), minced
> 2 Tablespoons dried thyme
> 2 Tablespoons ground allspice
> 1 teaspoon ground cinnamon
> 1 teaspoon ground nutmeg
> 4 cloves garlic, chopped

2 onions, chopped

1 bunch green onions, chopped

1 2" piece of fresh ginger, peeled and minced

2 Tablespoons Brown sugar

2 Tablespoons Kosher salt

2 Tablespoons ground black pepper

1/2 cup olive oil

1/4 cup soy sauce

1/2 cup orange juice

1/2 cup white vinegar

Mix all ingredients (besides pork!) in blender or food processor. Rub all over pork roast and marinate from 2 hours to overnight – the longer the marinade, the deeper the flavor. Grill on low to medium heat (300°) for 45-60 minutes or until pork registers 150°. Slice across the grain and serve with *festival* or cornbread (to soak up the heat!) Serves 16.

PUSSER'S PAINKILLER

In 1999 we entertained our family on St. John in the U.S. Virgin Islands. We had a large villa with pool, hot tub, huge patio, guest cottage, and many bedrooms. It overlooked the lovely Great Cruz Bay below. On the four evenings we did not dine in, each family treated to a gourmet dinner in a local restaurant. It was a wonderful week! We often began our meal with a round of this Caribbean drink. Mmmm.

Without ice, blend, shake or stir:

1 ounce cream of coconut

1 ounce orange juice

4 ounces pineapple juice

2 ounces Pusser's Rum

Pour into a big glass filled with ice and grate fresh nutmeg on top.

SHERYL TUSCH, HUDSONVILLE, MICHIGAN

Editor's Note: The original recipe for the Painkiller is said to come from the Soggy Dollar Bar, a little open-air bar on the beach of White Bay, on Jost Van Dyke, BVI. The Soggy Dollar gets its name from the fact that most of its patrons come not from the island but from their boats moored off shore. They wade through the water and present their now "soggy dollars" to the bartender in exchange for one of these beauties. If you're ever in the British Virgin Islands, don't miss this landmark or Jost Van Dyke's other famed institution, Foxy's. I dare you not to have fun.

Mexico

Like its North and South American counterparts, Mexico has a modern cuisine that is a combination of native ingredients blended with imports that occurred after the arrival of Europeans in the late 15th century –what has come to be termed the "Columbian Exchange." Certain ingredients are key to Mestizo and Mayan cuisine, primarily corn, tomatoes and chiles. Corn was first domesticated in Mexico, at roughly the same time rice was cultivated in Asia and wheat arose in Europe. An Aztec myth says that an ant discovered the essential maize on a volcano named Tonacatepetl. When the god Quetzalcoatl asked the lowly ant where he got it, the ant hesitated to share the information, but in the end relented and told the god where to find it. For his honesty, the ant was rewarded with other varieties of corn, and beans as well. Tortillas were quickly adapted from corn as a quick and portable food source.

While the tomato was first developed in the Andes, it was the Aztecs that gave it its modern name: the Aztec tomatl comes from the Mayan tomahu. The tomato took on several other titles upon its arrival in Europe, including the romantic "love apple" used by the French, or *pomme d'amour*, and *pomodoro* in Italy, which becomes "golden apple." Both of these were simply mispronunciations of the Spanish *pomo de moro*, or Moorish apple.

Because the tomato, like its cousin the potato, is a member of the belladonna family, Europeans initially were hesitant to use it for fear of it being poisonous, like its other cousin, the deadly nightshade. We've come a long way since then, and today there are more than 4,000 varieties of tomato. Regarding the fruit versus vegetable argument: you can call a tomato anything you like in my opinion, but shortly before 1900 the U.S. Supreme Court actually defined it as a vegetable, although this decision was motivated by potential tax benefits (at the time there was a tariff on vegetables, not on fruits).

CHICKEN MOLÉ

Mole is an Aztec creation, and comes from the Nahuatl word for mixture. It is a flavorful sauce combining roasted chilies and bitter chocolate, and is traditionally mixed in molcajetes, three-legged stone bowls that are similar in shape to the mortar and pestle.

This recipe comes from one of my sister Lisa's *three* cookbooks. I have made this dish innumerable times: when we attended Westminster Presbyterian Church in Grand Rapids, Michigan, it was my standard dish for new moms. Westminster had a circle of volunteers who would coordinate at least three meals for families just home from the hospital with newborn babies. Since we had three boys in short order, I was both cook and beneficiary of this program and appreciated it very much! It's a great dish for preparing ahead of time, then baking when you need it.

Since it's hard to find whole chickens cut up at stores in Calgary, I usually just grab a package of breasts and a package of thighs and call it good. As long as you have a blend of white and dark meat on the bone, you can really use any combination. Dried ancho chilies are also hard to find up here (sigh) so I substitute ancho chili powder when necessary.

1 4-5 pound chicken, cut up
1 large can diced tomatoes
1 1-ounce square bittersweet or unsweetened chocolate, shaved
1 Tablespoon ancho chili powder or 1 dried ancho chili, sliced into strips
1 Tablespoon dried oregano leaves
1 teaspoon ground black pepper
1 teaspoon salt
1 1/4 cups water
black beans and rice, or tortillas (optional)

Preheat oven to 450°. Place chicken pieces in one or two 9 x 13" pans. Pour tomatoes over chicken, then sprinkle on seasonings and chocolate. Pour water over all, and bake for 35 minutes, turning chicken once and stirring melted chocolate into pan sauce. Turn chicken once more and bake for 15 more minutes or until chicken is cooked. Serve with black beans and rice, or allow chicken to cool slightly then pull meat from the chicken, stir into sauce and serve in warmed tortillas.

CHILAQUILES

This is good to use when you have leftover chicken broth and a bit of chicken.

4-6 Tablespoons cooking oil
10 tortillas, cut in eighths
1 medium onion, minced
1 green pepper, diced (optional)
2-3 cloves garlic, minced
4-5 fresh tomatoes, diced *or* 2 1/2 cups canned tomatoes *or* 1 1/4 cups tomato puree mixed with 1 1/4 cups meat stock or chicken soup

salt and pepper to taste
1/2 pound grated Monterey Jack cheese

Heat oil in skillet and fry tortilla sections. Remove tortillas from pan, drain and set aside. To the oil that is left in the pan, add onion, green pepper, tomatoes and sauté. Season to taste with salt and pepper, and cover skillet and cook for 15 minutes to blend flavors.

Layer the fried tortillas and the cheese until all is used. Pour the sauce over all. Chilaquiles can be made either in a skillet on top of the stove using a low flame, or in a greased baking pan in the oven. Cook until well heated and cheese is melted, approximately 20 minutes.

CARLA STERK, CHIAPAS, MEXICO

ENCHILADAS SUIZAS

This dish gets its name (Swiss enchiladas) from the cheese and cream used in the sauce. The recipe is from a Missionary Aviation pilot's wife, Janet Walker, and I've had it for years. We often make it in Chiapas for visiting U.S. guests since it has ingredients that aren't too foreign to the American palate.

2 Tablespoons oil
1 onion, chopped
1 clove garlic, crushed
2 cups tomato puree
2 cans chopped green chiles (optional – can add any type of chile or taco sauce)
2 cups cooked chopped chicken
salt to taste
oil for frying
12 tortillas
6 chicken bouillon cubes

3 cups half and half
1/2 pound grated Monterey Jack cheese

Heat oil in saucepan and sauté onion until soft. Add garlic, tomato puree, chiles and chicken. Season with salt and simmer 10 minutes.

Fry tortillas in about 1 inch of hot oil; do not let them get crisp.

In saucepan, warm half and half and dissolve bouillon. Dip each tortilla in bouillon mixture, cover well with chicken mixture and roll up.

Arrange in baking dish and pour remaining half and half over filled tortillas. Top with cheese. Bake at 350° for 30 minutes or until cheese begins to brown. Serves 6.

CARLA STERK, CHIAPAS, MEXICO

LUPE OCAMPO'S PASTEL DE FLAN / CUSTARD DESSERT

Lupe Ocampo is the wife of the Mexican medical missionary who works with us in Chiapas. She made this for the visiting group from the United States who accompanied our son this summer, and was delighted that I would be interested in using her recipe in the U.S.

1 chocolate cake mix
8 eggs
2 cans sweetened condensed milk
2 cans evaporated milk
2 teaspoons vanilla
1 small jar of cajeta (Mexican caramel found in Mexican stores)
nuts and cherries for decoration (optional)

Preheat oven to 350°. Make the cake mix according to directions on package. Set aside. Spray a large ring shaped pan well with cooking spray. Pour a thin covering of cajeta in the bottom of the sprayed pan (if cajeta won't pour, place it briefly in the microwave). Pour the cake batter over the cajeta.

Mix the milks, eggs, and vanilla in a blender and slowly pour over the cake batter. The cake will come to the surface and the flan will go to the bottom. Bake for about 50-60 minutes. As soon as it comes out of the oven, invert it on a serving plate and decorate as desired with nuts and cherries.

The recipe can be cut in half and placed in a bundt pan if you only want to serve 8-10 people. Then use half of the cake mix to make something like cupcakes.

CARLA STERK, CHIAPAS, MEXICO

MAYAN INDIAN CHICKEN SOUP

Eating together for the Mayans is an important way to show your acceptance and respect for someone, and they are very hospitable hosts. We have often been treated to their best while they eat last to insure that everyone has as much as they want, even if that means there is not sufficient left for the members of the household. This soup is the most typical meal to serve to guests.

One chicken, cut up
1 cup chopped onion
1 cup chopped celery
1 cup chopped tomato
1/2 teaspoon dried thyme, or 1 1/2 teaspoons fresh thyme
Fried Rice (see below)
Tortillas, warmed

Cover chicken with water and bring to a boil (Mayans use more water so they have more broth, or caldo). After water boils, add onion, celery, tomato and thyme. Cook until done and serve with fried rice and warmed tortillas. This can also be put in a slow cooker on very low so it doesn't fall apart during the day.

CARLA STERK, CHIAPAS, MEXICO

MEXICAN FRIED RICE

This recipe is more Mayan. The Mayan Indians would think it was hilarious that I've put some of their recipes in writing because they never use cookbooks or written recipes.

1-2 Tablespoons oil
1-2 cups rice
1 onion, chopped
1 tomato, chopped
1 green pepper, chopped
2-4 cups water
1 cup frozen carrots and peas (optional)

Heat oil and stir in rice. Stir until rice is just a bit browned. Towards the end of cooking time, add onion, tomato and green pepper and sauté all together for a few minutes. Add twice as much water as the amount of the rice you started with (4 cups water to 2 cups rice, for example), peas and carrots if using, then cover and simmer on low heat until water is fully absorbed. Don't stir the rice while it is cooking.

CARLA STERK, CHIAPAS, MEXICO

SANGRIA

We enjoyed this beverage whenever we have visited Mexico and tried to duplicate its tang and fruity flavor. This recipe comes closest. We served this first at a
Cinco de Mayo party with a Mexican menu for our bridge club.

2 750-ml bottles of Zinfandel wine
3 cups cranberry-apple juice cocktail
1 cup orange juice
1 cup sugar
1 small apple, cored and sliced
2 oranges, sliced

Combine the first 4 ingredients in a punch bowl or large pitcher. Stir well to
dissolve sugar. Add fruit slices. Cover and refrigerate at least 2 and up to 8
hours. Serve with lots of ice.

SHERYL TUSCH, HUDSONVILLE, MICHIGAN

TORTILLAS

Editor's Note: Today's modern American army has perfected the MRE, or Meal
Ready to Eat. These individually packaged hot meals that do not require refrigeration are increasingly becoming part of the American lexicon, through media
exposure of Hurricane Katrina and the second Gulf War. Military researchers
continue to improve upon MREs, and are even researching ways for tomorrow's
soldier to be able to go without food altogether – perhaps a patch, similar to a nic-
otine patch, that would shoot nutrients directly into the soldier's system. Sound
like science fiction? Read Sarah Murray's *Moveable Feasts* if you don't believe me.

American military research scientists may turn out an impressive product, but
they can't lay claim to the invention of the MRE – for that we can credit the
Aztecs. Easy to transport, easily eaten while walking, a vessel to carry other

foods, maize tortillas were the perfect foodstuff for an army on the move. Turns out the rest of us kind of feel the same way – now you can find tortillas as easily as sliced bread. However, if you want to try your hand at the old fashioned homemade variety, here is a recipe from someone who certainly knows her way around a Mexican kitchen.

5 pounds all-purpose flour
2 Tablespoons salt
2 Tablespoons baking powder
2/3 cup solid vegetable shortening
5 1/4 cups hot tap water

Mix all dry ingredients for about ten minutes. Add shortening and mix thoroughly with hands until it resembles fine crumbs (about 15-20 minutes). Add water one cup at a time, pulling out clumps and setting aside. Once all clumps are pulled out, knead together for about 20 minutes. Place dough in a large resealable plastic bag, and let sit for 20 minutes.

Pinch 1-2 inch balls of dough, depending on how big a tortilla you want to make. Roll out to a circle shape. Makes 80-120 5-6" tortillas.

Noemi Cervantes Raeside, Grand Rapids, Michigan

United States of America, by Region

California

Can I just say, God bless Alice Waters. From the humble beginnings of her restaurant Chez Panisse in Berkeley, California, her idea of using seasonal, organic ingredients supplied by local farmers and ranchers has taken this planet by storm. What used to be referred to as "California cuisine" is now taking shape as the new way to eat and buy food. Consumers are demanding locally grown, organic foods in unprecedented numbers. It's a simple idea, really. Amazing it seemed like such a novel concept for so long.

Ms. Waters has taken this idea of reconnecting what we eat with where it came from, and created a school lunch program called The Edible Schoolyard. Students grow foods from seed, maintain the garden, harvest the food, cook it and share it with others.

To have a California-style dinner party, use seasonal ingredients, eat outside if weather allows, and keep the wine flowing! One recipe not in this section I'd recommend is the Beet and Goat Cheese Salad in the Canada section – it's a great medium for showing off that seasonal produce.

GAME HENS STUFFED WITH GRAPES AND WILD MUSHROOMS

These are so beautiful for a dinner party, easy for family, and are loaded with flavor. When we went to Calistoga this fall, the one stop I had to make was at the "Sattui" vineyard. Not for the wine, but for the Madeira. They're the only vineyard that only sells their Madeira at the vineyard, and it's heavenly. Usually served as an after-dinner wine, the Madeira lends itself to luscious flavors with poultry. Once you try this, you'll know what I mean. If you've not yet cooked with Madeira, do yourself a favor and give it a try. You'll not go back to just using "stock" for basting. I've served these for girls' night, parents, friends, and this year, Kieran may even make them for Christmas dinner. Keep your fingers crossed, cuz' that's what I'm hoping for!

1 cup Madeira
2 ounces dried cepes, porcini or morel mushrooms
1 cup seedless green or red grapes, cut in halves
8 Tablespoons butter, at room temperature
1/2 cup seasoned dried breadcrumbs
2 Tablespoons chopped fresh parsley
1/4 teaspoon dried thyme
4 Cornish game hens
salt and freshly ground black pepper

Bring Madeira to a boil in a small saucepan. Add the mushrooms, remove from heat and set aside. Preheat oven to 350°.

Combine the grapes, 4 Tablespoons of butter, bread crumbs, parsley, and thyme in a mixing bowl and toss well.

Rinse the hens and pat them dry. Fill the cavities with the stuffing. Drain the mushrooms, reserving the Madeira, and place one mushroom in each cavity. Place the stuffed birds in a roasting pan. Dot with remaining butter and sprinkle them with salt and pepper. Pour a small amount of the reserved Madeira (about 1/3 cup) into the pan. Bake for 1 hour, basting occasionally.

Remove the pan from the oven, and transfer the hens to a heated platter. Add the remaining mushrooms and Madeira to the pan, and cook over low heat until the liquid is slightly reduced, about 5 minutes. Pour the sauce over the hens, and serve immediately.

LISA MALONEY, BOULDER, COLORADO

QUICK AND EASY CHILI – CALIFORNIA STYLE

This recipe came from a family that owns a restaurant in Orange County, California. We use this recipe each winter for the annual Newport Harbor Festival of Lights Boat Parade. We were fortunate for two years to be in the parade and we served this chili on the boat for our "Boat Parade Party." Now we watch the parade from the beach, and this is a California tradition for us!

1 pound package of ground beef or ground turkey
1 large can each of pinto beans and kidney beans
1 small-medium can of garbanzo beans
1-2 large cans of stewed tomatoes
1 large onion
Seasonings – salt, pepper, red pepper flakes for spicy chili

Cook the meat in a pan with seasonings, place in a pot after (drain the grease before putting in pot). Chop up onion and sauté in a pan, place in the pot with meat. Add all cans of beans, drain all cans before adding beans to pot.

Add large can of stewed tomatoes, juice and all. You can use two cans if you need more juice in the chili.

Bring to a boil and let cook on low-medium heat for one-two hours or so. Top with cheese, serve with cornbread. It is a great dish for a lot of people. You can double the recipe with a larger group. Enjoy!

Julie Rohrer, Castle Rock, Colorado

Midwest / West Michigan

I am loathe to describe the natural beauty and hospitality of West Michigan, for fear that those reading this may spread the word and millions of people will discover our little secret. But, like our first President, I cannot tell a lie. When I think of west Michigan, I can feel the breeze coming off Lake Michigan, and the sun shining on my face as I curl my toes in the warm sand of the beaches that line its shores. I smell an intoxicating mixture of lake water, dune grass, and sand. I hear the crunch of dead leaves and twigs under my feet while I hike through North Manitou Island, munching on gorp made with dried cherries. I take in the eternity of the water before me as I sit and watch the waves on Lake Michigan. Honestly, I could do that for hours. It makes me laugh when I think of all the people outside of Michigan who have asked me "so... can you *see* across it?"

West Michigan gets its own special section in this book because so many of those contributing to it come from this area and have the same fond memories I do (you'll notice several recipes are from Sheryl Tusch – thanks Mom!). We always want what we can't have, and my poor neighbors here in Canada have had to suffer through my pining for fresh Michigan cherries and – is it really too much to ask? – plain Hershey bars for my s'mores during camping season. Many of the recipes in this section have been shared again and again at potlucks, family gatherings, high school graduations, showers, and funerals. Babies are born, kids graduate from college, grandparents pass away. Time marches on. When everything else is unpredictable in this world, I can still count on these simple gifts: my great-aunties' pies, my mother's spare ribs, the unabashed decadence of Texas sheet cake, cherries picked right from the tree, maple syrup still hot from the sugar shack. Ché Guevara was right: homesickness does begin with food.

Appetizers, Beverages and Snacks

BLACK BEAN AND MANGO DIP

This dip is best prepared on a warm summer's day, while quaffing a Bell's Two-Hearted Ale in anticipation of good friends coming over for euchre. A friend of the family, Debbie Bowling, introduced me to this recipe during one of those warm, lazy summer days on the shores of Lake Michigan. Ripe mangoes and lots of cilantro contribute to making this dip both delicious and colorful.

   8 ounces cream cheese, softened
   1/2 cup sour cream
   2 Tablespoons taco seasoning
   1 can black beans, drained and rinsed
   1 bunch cilantro, chopped
   1 jalapeño pepper, minced
   2-3 scallions, chopped
   1 mango, diced
   1 red pepper, diced

Mix cream cheese, sour cream and taco seasoning together. Spread on bottom of serving dish. Spread black beans on top of cream cheese mixture. Mix remaining ingredients together and layer on top of dip.

Beth Heckman, Ada, Michigan

CRACKER CRITTERS

A fun snack for grownups and children both!

3 cups animal crackers
2 cups chocolate flavored bear-shaped mini-grahams
1 6-ounce package fish-shaped cheese crackers
2 cups miniature pretzels
2 cups honey roasted peanuts

Combine in large container with a tight fitting lid.

Sheryl Tusch, Hudsonville, Michigan

DRIED CHERRY GORP

1 cup oat cereal
1 cup dried cherries
1/4 cup banana chips
1/4 cup raisins
1/4 cup dried apple chips, slightly crushed
1/4 cup cashews
1/4 cup peanuts
1/4 cup salted sunflower seeds
1/4 cup coconut, toasted

Mix all together carefully in an airtight container. For little ones, the smallest plastic bags are a perfect size for toting Gorp. Makes about 4 cups.

SHERYL TUSCH, HUDSONVILLE, MICHIGAN

JEZEBEL SAUCE

This is a colorful hors d'oeuvre to serve at a party. One of the last times I made it, I shared it at cousin Ed and Linda Van Dam's lovely home near Lake Michigan, where another cousin, George Vande Bunte, revved up our enthusiasm to visit Australia and New Zealand.

1 18-ounce jar pineapple preserves
1 12-ounce jar orange marmalade
1 9-ounce jar apple jelly
1 5-ounce jar horseradish, drained
1 1.2-ounce can dry mustard
1 Tablespoon coarse ground black pepper

Combine jams (I've used various proportions of the three preserves listed), horseradish, dry mustard, and pepper with a wire whisk. Pour over cream cheese and serve with crackers. The sauce keeps refrigerated up to 6 months. The recipe makes a lot—plenty to share with others!

SHERYL TUSCH, HUDSONVILLE, MICHIGAN

PEANUT BUTTER APPLE TREATS

This is a nutritious, fun-to-make-with-grandchildren type of snack, parent approved.

Cut three "donuts" or 8 "smile" wedges from a cored tart apple. Spread one side with peanut butter and top with crisped rice cereal, coconut, chopped nuts, or granola, or a combination of these.

Sheryl Tusch, Hudsonville, Michigan

PIÑA COLADA FRUIT DIP

This flavorful colorful tray is perfect for parties. It always reminds me of being in sunny Hawaii. Aloha!

    1 8-ounce can crushed pineapple
    3/4 cup milk
    1 3 1/2 ounce package instant coconut pudding mix
    1/2 cup sour cream or nonfat yogurt
    Assorted cut fresh fruit

Combine in blender. Pour in plastic bowl with a lid. Refrigerate several hours or overnight to blend flavors. Serve with assorted fresh fruits in a hollowed out pineapple,cut lengthwise.

Sheryl Tusch, Hudsonville, Michigan

PIÑA COLADA SLUSH

This is a very refreshing summer drink to have on hand for impromptu company or my son-in-law Adam. The recipe came from my cousin, Judy Heuvelhorst. We used to serve it often at our pool parties.

    1 can unsweetened pineapple juice
    1 12 ounce can frozen lemonade, undiluted
    1 can cream of coconut
    1 pint light rum

Mix well in a large container or pour into several smaller ones. Put in freezer for at least two days. Put one scoop in a glass, and fill the glass with 7-up.

SHERYL TUSCH, HUDSONVILLE, MICHIGAN

SUGARED NUTS

I have made this treat for countless Christmases and given them as gifts in assorted containers for many years. They are delicious!

1 cup sugar
5 Tablespoons water
1 Tablespoon cinnamon
1/2 teaspoon salt
3/4 pound pecans
3/4 pound walnuts

Combine in a heavy large pan. Boil. Add pecans and walnuts. Boil again. Remove from heat. Stir until well coated. Spread on buttered cookie sheet to dry.

SHERYL TUSCH, HUDSONVILLE, MICHIGAN

SUMMER SALSA

This is very similar to mango salsa, but the substitution of nectarines means you can use more local produce – plus locally grown nectarines (in my experience) tend to be more reliable in terms of taste and texture than the far-flung mango. A version of this recipe was given to me originally from Michelle Alster, who got it from a friend as well. Goes great with tortilla chips, or over grilled chicken or fish.

1 lime
3-5 nectarines, peeled and diced

1 red pepper, diced

1 jalapeño pepper, seeded and minced

1/2 cup diced red onion

2 Tablespoons chopped fresh cilantro

2 Tablespoons red wine vinegar

Grate the zest of the lime, and squeeze the juice into a bowl. Toss everything else in, mix together and serve. How easy is that?

Breakfast and Breads

[Breadbaking is] one of those almost hypnotic businesses, like a dance from some ancient ceremony. It leaves you filled with one of the world's sweetest smells.... there is no chiropractic treatment, no Yoga exercise, no hour of meditation in a music-throbbing chapel, that will leave you emptier of bad thoughts than this homely ceremony of making bread.

~M.F.K. Fisher, The Art of Eating

BUTTERMILK QUICK BREAD

This is a great mix to have on hand for a quick treat.

1 14-ounce box of bran flakes with raisins

4 1/2 cups flour

2 3/4 cups sugar

2 teaspoons salt

4 cups buttermilk or 3 cups plain yogurt with 1 cup milk

1 cup vegetable oil

4 eggs, beaten

1/2 cup dried fruit (chopped apricots, dates, cherries or sweetened cranberries)

1/2 cup chopped walnuts

Combine dry ingredients in a large bowl and set aside. Combine buttermilk, oil and eggs and pour into dry ingredients. Stir until just blended.

Keep in refrigerator, tightly sealed, for up to two weeks. When ready to bake, spoon into a greased and floured 9 x 5 inch loaf pan (batter will be thick). Bake at 325° for 1 hour and 15 minutes or until a knife inserted in the middle comes out dry. Makes three loaves.

RUTH BOSS, HUDSONVILLE, MICHIGAN

CARAMEL COFFEECAKE

…or "sticky buns" which most of the Cole family calls this delicious recipe. It disappears fast and can be eaten anytime. We serve it at brunch for holidays, and take it camping already made. It's good hot or cold. We've made it for dessert, too!

2 10-count cans refrigerated biscuit dough

3/4 cup brown sugar

4 Tablespoons butter, melted

1/3 cup maple syrup

1/3 cup chopped pecans

18 ounces cream cheese, softened

2 Tablespoons butter, melted

Grease two 9" x 13" pans, and preheat oven to 350°. Mix brown sugar, 4 Tablespoons of butter, maple syrup, and pecans and spread in the bottom of one of the pans. In a separate bowl, mix together cream cheese and 2 Tablespoons of butter. Place one Tablespoon of cream cheese filling in each biscuit, fold in half and lay on top of syrup mixture. Continue until all biscuits are used and pan is filled.

Bake for 25 minutes or until golden brown. Remove from oven and invert the empty baking pan on top of hot coffeecake, and carefully flip over so the good stuff is on top now. I usually use two oven mitts and flip it fast. It's wonderful – enjoy!

SHAWN COLE, GRAND RAPIDS, MICHIGAN

DATE BREAD

This recipe needs no shortening. The recipe came from Dena Yntema, my grandmother, best known for her white bread and cinnamon rolls served every Saturday afternoon.

Put 1 cup dates, finely diced, into 1 cup of boiling water. Let stand until cool.

Mix:
1 egg
1 cup sugar
1 teaspoon soda
2 cups flour
2 teaspoon baking powder
1/2 cup nuts
1/3 teaspoon salt

Add dates and liquid. Bake in a slow oven about 45-60 minutes.

SHERYL TUSCH, HUDSONVILLE, MICHIGAN

ELLIOTT'S FAMOUS CHOCOLATE PANCAKES

Editor's Note: these were created by my son Elliott, who was very eager to help me on this project. The recipe is wholly his own, and was one of the first created for the cookbook. A budding chef, that boy!

2 cups flour
2 teaspoons baking powder
1/2 teaspoon salt
1 cup milk
2/3 cup nonfat vanilla yogurt
1/3 cup water
2 eggs
1/8 cup oil
1/8 cup chocolate sauce

Toppings:
Granola
Yogurt
Sliced bananas
Chocolate sauce

Blend first three ingredients. Stir together remaining ingredients in a separate bowl, and mix into flour mixture. Grease griddle or large pan with butter or oil and heat. Pour pancake batter onto hot pan by 1/3 cupfuls. Make 18 pancakes, and enjoy!

Elliott Niemur, Calgary, Alberta

GRANDMA VANDE BUNTE'S WHITE BREAD

Having grown up across the road from my future mother-in-law, I knew a lot about her prowess of baking bread almost weekly. Amazingly, I ended up marrying her son Ed, and continued enjoying her bread. She always told me it was her mother's recipe that she made. When our first daughter was born I decided to be a stay-at-home mom and thought that making bread would be fun. I asked my mother-in-law, Marian Van Dam, if she would teach me how to make Grandma Vande Bunte's bread. We spent a day making bread and I was off and running with it. Our second daughter, Jane, came along and I continued the bread making for many years. Jane was so hooked on the homemade bread that when she would go over to a friend's for a play date she would bring two slices of bread in a small baggie with her for her sandwich. She would have nothing to do with store bought bread! Her friends' mothers were real champs and just smiled when Jane came with her own baggie of homemade bread. Occasionally she would bring a whole loaf to share!

1 cup warm water
2 Tablespoons sugar
3 packages dry yeast
1 Tablespoon salt
1 cup of scalded milk
3 cups of hot water
1+ cups of flour

Mix the warm water, 1 Tablespoon of the sugar and the yeast together in a small bowl. Set aside and let mixture come to a nice foamy rise.

Combine remaining sugar, salt, milk and hot water in a large bowl. Allow it to cool down enough so that when you add the yeast mixture it won't be so hot as to kill the yeast. When it has cooled down, add the yeast mixture and begin adding white flour 1 cup at a time. Stir the flour in with a whisk until too thick to do so. Begin stirring with a wooden spoon until you no longer are able to. At this point, flour your counter and plop the dough mixture on top. Knead in the additional flour until it has a nice smooth texture as you are working with it. Let the dough rise in a large pan or bowl, approximately one to two hours, in a warm place. It will completely fill the pan to the top. Cover it with a towel as it rises. Grease 5 bread pans. When it has risen, separate the dough into 5 loaves and place in the prepared pans. Cover with towel and let rise again until they are nice loaf sizes. Preheat oven to 350°. Place loaves in preheated oven and bake for approximately 30 minutes or until nicely browned. The bread freezes well and it is a real treat to pull a fresh loaf of bread out when needed!

LINDA VAN DAM, HOLLAND, MICHIGAN

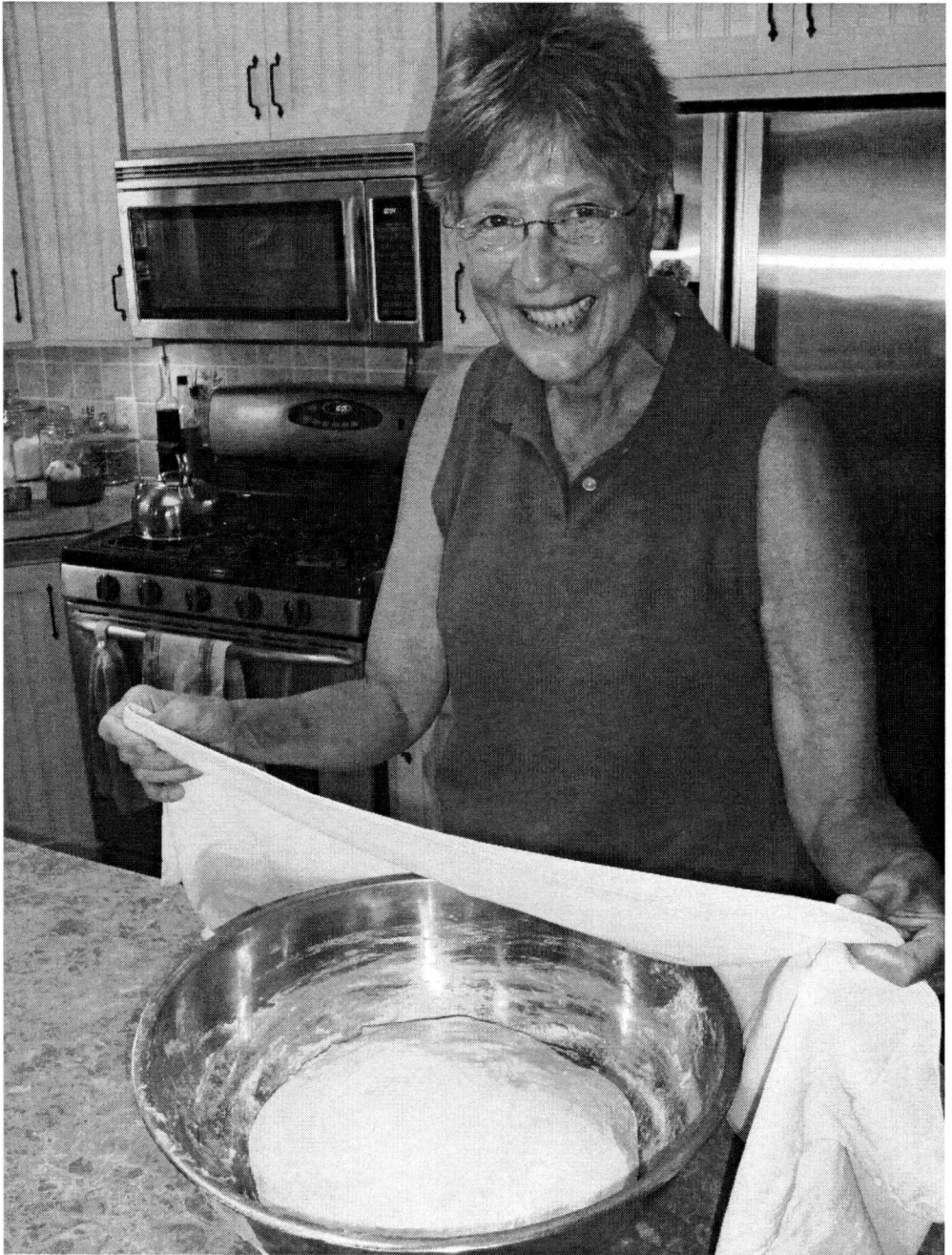

Linda Van Dam, making Grandma Vande Bunte's White Bread.

HERP'S BLUEBERRY MUFFINS

When my children were small we took them to Herpolsheimer's department store in Grand Rapids at Christmas time to see Santa and ride the small train that circled a large room way up at ceiling height. These muffins served with a glass of cold milk in the lovely tearoom were a perfect conclusion to the afternoon.

4 Tablespoons butter, room temperature
1/2 cup sugar
1 cup milk
2 eggs, well beaten
3 scant cups flour
2 teaspoons baking powder
2 cups fresh blueberries, dredged in flour
sugar for sprinkling

In a large mixing bowl, cream butter and sugar. Add milk and eggs, blending well. Stir in flour and baking powder. Gently fold in blueberries. Fill greased muffin tins 2/3 full. Top each muffin with 1/2 tsp. sugar. Bake at 350 degrees for 30 minutes. Makes about 18 muffins.

SHERYL TUSCH, HUDSONVILLE, MICHIGAN

Editor's Note: For those who may have not been in Grand Rapids in the 1970's, Herpolsheimer's may still sound familiar: it is featured in the film *The Polar Express*. Chris Van Allsburg, the book's author and illustrator, is originally from Grand Rapids, Michigan.

LIONEL'S PECAN-CINNAMON STICKY BUNS

This recipe is based on one found years ago in a magazine, but Lionel added extra ingredients (most notably the rum raisins), and boy oh boy are they delicious.... I believe he's brought them to both Yntema and VandeBunte parties, as well as countless other potlucks. They are always a hit!

This is quite a complicated looking recipe, but trust me....these are the BEST sticky buns you will ever eat – it is well worth the effort.

Dough
1 Tablespoon sugar
2 envelopes active dry yeast
1/4 cup warm water
1/3 cup sugar
3 eggs
1 1/2 teaspoon salt
1 teaspoon vanilla
3/4 cup whole milk (don't get all healthy and substitute skim here)
1/2 cup (1 stick) unsalted butter, melted
5 1/4 – 5 3/4 cups all purpose flour

Cinnamon-Sugar Filling
1/2 cup packed light or dark brown sugar
1/2 cup sugar
2 teaspoons ground cinnamon
3/4 cup coarsely chopped pecans, toasted
2/3 cup raisins, soaked in spiced rum at LEAST overnight*
3 Tablespoons unsalted butter, melted

Caramel-Pecan Topping
3/4 cup packed dark brown sugar
1/2 cup unsalted butter

1/4 cup VandeBunte maple syrup (or other brand, if you must)
1/4 teaspoon salt
1 1/2 cup pecan halves or large pieces, toasted
Reserved rum from soaked raisins

For rum raisins: put raisins in a container and add enough spiced rum to cover them. If you forgot to do this, or don't have time, you can also put the rum and raisins in a small saucepan, and warm them up over low heat until raisins are hydrated (15 minutes or so). Either way, drain the raisins, and add to filling. DON'T DISCARD THE RUM – see topping section.

To prepare the dough....

In a small bowl, dissolve the 1 Tablespoon of sugar and yeast in the warm water. Gently stir once, and let stand five minutes or until bubbly. Using a wooden spoon, combine the 1/3 cup sugar, eggs, salt, vanilla, milk, 1/2 cup melted butter, and foamy yeast mixture. Blend until smooth. Add the flour 1/2 cup at a time, until well combined. When most of the flour is added, turn out onto your counter and start kneading the dough until smooth and elastic – 3-5 minutes.

Lightly butter a large bowl. Gather dough and turn into a ball, coating all sides with the butter. Cover the bowl with plastic, set aside in a warm spot to rise until doubled in bulk, about 1 1/2 hours.

To prepare the filling....

In a small bowl combine sugars, cinnamon and pecans. Stir in raisins (don't forget to RESERVE THE RUM!), set aside. Reserve 3 Tablespoons butter.

To prepare the topping....

In a medium saucepan combine brown sugar, butter, reserved rum, maple syrup and salt. Bring to boiling over medium heat; reduce heat and simmer 1-2 minutes until well combined. Meanwhile, butter 2 - 9" baking pans (or one 11 x 14 pan). Sprinkle half the pecans in the bottom of each pan. Drizzle the caramel topping over the pecans in each pan. Set aside to cool.

When dough has doubled, punch it down then let it rest 10 minutes. Roll out the dough to a 14 x 24 inch rectangle. Spread the reserved 3 Tablespoons butter over the surface of the dough. Sprinkle the cinnamon-sugar filling over the butter, gently pressing the mixture into the dough. Starting at the short end of the dough, roll it up. Seal the seam by pinching the dough together. Cut into 12 slices, about 1 inch thick each. Place the slices, cut side down, onto the caramel topping in each pan.

Cover both pans with plastic, let pans stand in a warm place until doubled, about an hour. OR...chill overnight, let stand at room temperature about an hour before baking, they will surprisingly rise quite well overnight in the fridge.

When ready to bake, center the oven rack. Place an extra pan below to catch any drips from the caramel sauce, in case it spills over. Bake at 350° for 30-35 minutes, covering the rolls with foil for the last 10 minutes to prevent overbrowning.

Cool in baking pan 5 minutes, then invert onto a serving platter. Enjoy warm or at room temperature. These will keep well if covered for 2 days, but they never seem to last that long.

CINDY LOZA, MARION, IOWA

LOW-ALTITUDE PANCAKES

Whenever I make these pancakes, I remember the time I brought all the ingredients to the Maloney home for a family get-together special treat. Well....I couldn't get them to rise or brown! All they did was stick to the non-stick Teflon pan. I ruined Lisa's skillet trying desperately to serve my special treat! Then someone asked me if I had adjusted the recipe for the altitude in Colorado. Why would this Michigan cook have known to do that?

    1 cup buttermilk
    1 egg
    1 teaspoon baking soda
    1 teaspoon baking powder
    1/2 to 3/4 cups of flour

Mix the first four ingredients well and let stand for five minutes. Add flour just to combine. Bake on hot griddle, turn only once, 'til golden brown. Drop on some Michigan blueberries, pecans, or banana slices, if desired. Serve with maple syrup from the Vande Bunte Sap Shack! Makes about five pancakes.
SHERYL TUSCH, HUDSONVILLE, MICHIGAN

OVERNIGHT FRENCH TOAST

This is not from a foreign country—unless you count "French" bread! We served this at my daughter Lisa's wedding breakfast in a cottage near Ottawa Beach in Holland, Michigan, with sausages kept hot in a crockpot with cranberry sauce. Add Vande Bunte Maple Syrup and fresh fruit—what a happy memory!

    1 loaf French bread, unsliced
    8 eggs
    1 cup whole milk
    1/2 cup butter

2/3 cup brown sugar

1/2 teaspoon cinnamon

Cut bread into 1 1/2 inch slices. Combine milk and beaten eggs. Pour in a cookie sheet with sides. Put slices of bread on top. Turn over after five minutes. Butter another cookie sheet. Melt butter, brown sugar and cinnamon in microwave. Pour into buttered cookie sheet. Put soaked bread on top. Bake 25 minutes at 350° or put pan, covered with foil, into refrigerator and bake the following morning, uncovered.

SHERYL TUSCH, HUDSONVILLE, MICHIGAN

SOUR CREAM COFFEE CAKE

We married and left Michigan in '57 for my husband's new job with Esso Research and Engineering in New Jersey. A few years later he and another Esso friend originally from Pennsylvania were sent on a job to Leonard Refinery in Alma, Michigan. We wives went along and after a few days in a motel, we found a cottage to rent on a nearby lake where we could cook. For the first meal, we decided to pull out all the stops; roast beef, mashed potatoes, gravy, vegetables, and apple pie for dessert. That sounded great to the guys, who were working split shifts at the time. Good plan except that Ruth Ann, Chuck and I enjoyed it for dinner, while Robert got it warmed up for breakfast. He tried hard, but it was just too much to deal with at 7:00 a.m. We had a great time in Alma and tried out all of the local eateries. Sometimes we dined out at a local diner and had the most exquisite strawberry/rhubarb pie. Or we went to The Embers in Mt. Pleasant and enjoyed a most interesting side of green peas and peanuts. I tried for years to make that dish and never came close. Another place we went was a restaurant in an old house that we called the Duck Farm, a really nice place featuring home cooking and duck, of course. The following is a recipe for a delicious coffee cake that Ruth Ann made and wrote out for me. The card is yellowed now and covered with splotches of batter, but it's still legible and I always think of Ruth Ann when I make it and I always get compliments when I serve it.

1/4 pound margarine
1 cup sugar
2 eggs
1 cup sour cream
1 teaspoon vanilla
2 cups flour
1/2 teaspoon salt
1 teaspoon baking powder
1 teaspoon baking soda

Topping:
1/2 cup brown sugar
1/2 cup chopped walnuts or pecans
1 teaspoon cinnamon

Mix topping ingredients and set aside. Cream margarine and sugar until fluffy. Add eggs, sour cream, vanilla and beat again. Sift together and add flour, salt, baking powder, baking soda, and beat until smooth. Grease and flour a 10" tube or angel food cake pan. Spoon in a little less than half of the batter and smooth. Sprinkle half the topping on batter and spoon in the rest of the batter. Sprinkle with remaining topping. Bake at 350° about 45 minutes.

DEE TUSCH, MEDINA, TEXAS

Cookies and Bars

10 CUP COOKIES

Sandy Vander Laan baked these for my farewell party at Rogers Department store, where I had worked in the Courtesy Department for eight years. The recipe makes lots of cookies, and they freeze well.

    1 cup butter
    1 cup peanut butter
    1 cup brown sugar
    2 eggs
    1 cup flour
    1 teaspoon soda
    1/2 teaspoon baking powder
    1 cup coconut
    1 cup raisins
    2 cups chocolate chips
    1 cup nuts
    1 cup quick oatmeal

Cream butter, peanut butter, sugar, and eggs. Stir in flour, baking soda, and baking powder. Stir in rest of ingredients by hand. Drop on greased baking sheet. Bake at 350° for 10 to 20 minutes.

SHERYL TUSCH, HUDSONVILLE, MICHIGAN

ALMOND BARS

This recipe was given to me when I worked at Rogers Department Store by Nancy Hall shortly before she died. I always think of Nancy and my days at the Courtesy Desk when I make them.

1 cup butter, room temperature
1 1/4 to 1 1/2 cups almond paste (1/2 pound)
2 cups sugar
2 eggs
1/2 teaspoon salt (optional)
2 cups flour

Cream together the butter and almond paste. Beat in sugar and eggs. Add flour. Pour into greased 9 x 13 pan. Bake 40 minutes at 300°. They may be drizzled with frosting, but are delicious plain. Cut in small portions. They freeze and mail well and are a great Christmas cookie.

SHERYL TUSCH, HUDSONVILLE, MICHIGAN

ALMOND ROCA

This is a special family treat. I started making it when I was about 10 and have used it every Christmas for the last 30 years. It is easy and great. It is also a great gift to give.

1 cup butter (half pound)
1 cup white sugar
1/4 cup water
3/4 cup slivered (or halved) almonds
chocolate chips or baking chocolate

Set frying pan at highest heat and add all the ingredients. Have pan that you will pour it into ready. When bubbly all over, time 7 minutes (I don't time it, just look for the stuff to be almost burnt!). Stir constantly with a wooden spoon. It turns a dark brown and starts to smoke slightly (or a lot). Pour into a pizza pan or cookie sheet. Let harden. Wipe with a paper towel to get the grease off the top or the chocolate wont stick. Melt chocolate chips or chunks of Bernard Callebeaut chocolate in the microwave or over a double boiler and spread on top. Let harden. Break into pieces and try not to eat it all!!!

MICHELLE DEN HOED, CALGARY, ALBERTA

BRIGHT GREEN WREATH CHRISTMAS COOKIES

Be sure to make these cookies on a day when you are not going out at night, because your fingers will be green for a day! They are fun to make and serve on Christmas cookie trays, but are a bit messy to form.

    40 big marshmallows
    1 stick butter or margarine
    1 teaspoon vanilla
    2 teaspoons green food coloring
    4 cups corn flake cereal
    red cinnamon candies (optional)

Melt butter or margarine. Add marshmallows and melt. Remove from heat. Add vanilla and food coloring, and stir well. Mix in corn flakes. Drop on a cookie sheet lined with waxed paper and shape into about 20 wreaths. Cinnamon candies may be added for holly berries. Cover loosely with waxed paper and set aside for 2 days

SHERYL TUSCH, HUDSONVILLE, MICHIGAN

CARMEL LAYER SQUARES

My fun-loving cousin Marcia Datema brought these cookies to an Yntema cousin sleepover in Reed City one year and we all loved them. She was our best storyteller and remembered all the funky jokes from one year to the next. Whenever I am unwrapping all the caramels (the most time-consuming part!) I remember some of the hysterical nights playing cards until about 2:00 in the morning, snacking, and laughing until our sides hurt. We miss her still.

1 14 ounce package of light caramels (50)
1/3 cup evaporated milk
German chocolate cake mix
3/4 cup oleo
1/3 cup evaporated milk
1 cup nuts
1 cup chocolate chips

Unwrap and melt the caramels and 1/3 cup of evaporated milk over low heat.

Combine next four ingredients. Pat 1/2 the dough in an ungreased 9 x 13 pan. Bake at 350° for 6 minutes. Sprinkle on 1 cup of chocolate chips, then the melted caramel mixture. Drop the rest of the dough by spoonfuls and spread. Bake an additional 25 minutes. Store in refrigerator.

SHERYL TUSCH, HUDSONVILLE, MICHIGAN

CHURCH WINDOW COOKIES

This is another good cookie for a tray of Christmas treats. They do not take any baking time. My son-in-law Adam likes them, but I had been making them for many years before he was part of our family. Children love the look of the colored marshmallows.

1 cup chocolate chips
2 Tablespoons butter
1 cup powdered sugar
1 egg
1 teaspoon vanilla
1/2 cup chopped nuts
1/2 bag of colored marshmallows
coconut

Melt chips with butter in double boiler over hot water (or use a microwave). Add powdered sugar, egg, nuts, and vanilla. Mix thoroughly and remove from heat. Add marshmallows. Shape into a log on waxed paper. Roll in coconut. Chill and store in refrigerator. Slice as needed.

Sheryl Tusch, Hudsonville, Michigan

CRUNCHY CLUSTERS (BARS OR COOKIES)

These treats are sooo good, they are almost like candy. They make a nice contrast on a tray of cookies at Christmas time. The good quality white chocolate does seem to make a difference.

> 2 12 ounce packages of good quality white chocolate discs or chips
> 4 Tablespoons peanut butter
> 2 cups peanuts
> 2 1/2 cups crisped rice cereal
> 2 cups miniature marshmallows

Melt candy with peanut butter over a slow burner, stirring constantly so it doesn't burn. Cool slightly. Stir in peanuts, then cereal, then marshmallows, only to coat. Put in lightly buttered 9 x 13 pan or:

Drop on waxed paper. If in bars, cut before they are completely set. They will set at room temperature or if you're in a hurry, you can refrigerate them. Store at room temperature. They freeze well.

Sheryl Tusch, Hudsonville, Michigan

FRUIT PUNCH BARS

This recipe comes from my days at Sandy Hill School and I have been making them since 1972! They are sticky, so are best served with a fork on a plate—although classified as a "cookie."

2 eggs
1 1/2 cups sugar
1 16 ounce can fruit cocktail, undrained
2 1/4 cups flour
1 1/2 teaspoons baking soda
1 teaspoon vanilla
1/2 teaspoon salt
1 1/3 cups shredded coconut
1/2 cup chopped walnuts

Glaze:
3/4 cups sugar
1/2 cup butter
1/2 teaspoon vanilla
1/4 cup evaporated milk

For glaze, combine all in a small pan. Boil for 2 minutes, stirring constantly. Remove from heat and cool.

Generously grease and flour 15 x 10 inch jelly roll pan. Beat eggs and sugar at high speed. Stir in can of fruit cocktail. Add flour, baking soda, vanilla and salt and beat until well blended. Sprinkle on coconut and walnuts. Bake at 350° for 20 minutes. While hot, drizzle with glaze. Cut into bars.

SHERYL TUSCH, HUDSONVILLE, MICHIGAN

GRAHAM CRACKER COOKIES

Line a cookie sheet with graham crackers. Boil 1/2 cup brown sugar and 1/2 cup butter. Pour over and add as many chopped nuts as you like. Bake 10 minutes at 325°. Cut into rectangles based on graham cracker perforations.

These were a favorite of my children when they were small, and are easy to make. Another version of this cookie follows:

Line a jelly roll pan with aluminum foil, dull side up. Break cinnamon crisp graham crackers in half and line pan. Boil 3/4 cup butter and 3/4 cup sugar for 2 minutes and pour over crackers. Sprinkle top with 1 1/2 cups chopped nuts and a 6 ounce bag of Heath Bits o' Brickle bits. Bake for 15 minutes at 325°. Cool 10 to 15 minutes before cutting into squares. Cool before eating.

This second version involves a trip to the grocery store for the special crackers and Brickle bits. The first one is so handy because the ingredients are right in the cupboard!

SHERYL TUSCH, HUDSONVILLE, MICHIGAN

GRANDMA VANDE BUNTE'S DROP COOKIES

My brother-in-law, Robert Tusch, thought these were delicious treats, so I often make them when I know he is coming for a visit from Texas. And it's fun to make cookies that I know my grandmother made on the farm for her eight children to enjoy!

1 cup solid vegetable shortening
1 cup sugar
1 cup brown sugar
1 teaspoon vanilla
2 eggs

2 cups flour
1 teaspoon soda
1 teaspoon baking powder
2 cups oatmeal
2 cups rice crispies
1 cup coconut

Cream shortening and sugars. Add eggs and vanilla and mix well. Combine flour, soda, and baking powder and add. Stir in oatmeal, cereal and coconut mixing well after each addition. Bake for ten minutes at 350°.

Sheryl Tusch, Hudsonville, Michigan

GRANDMA VANDE BUNTE'S ICE BOX COOKIES

2 cups brown sugar
1 cup (2 sticks) butter, softened
2 eggs
1 Tablespoon vanilla
1 teaspoon salt
3 1/2 cups flour
2 teaspoon baking powder

Add ingredients in the order given and pack down in a meatloaf pan. Chill. Slice and bake as needed at 350° until lightly brown.

Sheryl Tusch, Hudsonville, Michigan

HENRI'S BUCKET FULL OF OATMEAL COOKIES

This recipe came from a family friend and is great when you want fresh cookies. Make the big mix and then just make a batch at a time.

In a large bowl or bucket combine:

1 1/2 cups sugar
1 1/2 cups brown sugar
3 cups flour (can use whole wheat)
2 teaspoons salt
2 teaspoons baking soda
1 teaspoon baking powder
Cut in 2 cups of shortening.
Add 6 cups of rolled oats.

Mix well, cover and store in cool place.

To make cookies:

Combine in bowl:

1 beaten egg
2 teaspoons vanilla
4 cups of the above mix

Mix well and drop onto greased cookie sheet. Bake at 350° for 12 minutes.

**Optional additions to cookies:
Nuts
Raisins
Cinnamon
Chocolate chips
MICHELLE DEN HOED, CALGARY, ALBERTA

PECAN SQUARES

We ate well at Sandy Hill School where I taught for many years. One day we had cookies for dessert at a potluck and Mike brought these bars. They taste like pecan pie! I assumed his wife had made them, but he had. They became a favorite to serve at Hope Village Square workshop meetings in the early 1990s at my church after an evening of crafting. They make good cookies to serve at Christmas, too.

Crust:
2/3 cup powdered sugar
2 cups flour
2 sticks softened butter (1 cup)

Sift flour and sugar together in a large bowl. Cut in butter until mixture forms fine crumbs. Pat into 9 x 13 greased pan. Bake for 20 minutes at 350°. Meanwhile, make topping:

Topping:
2/3 cup melted butter
1/2 cup honey
3 Tablespoons heavy cream
1/2 cup brown sugar
3 1/2 cups coarsely chopped pecans

Mix butter, honey, cream and brown sugar together. Stir in nuts, coating thoroughly. Spread over crust. Return to oven and bake 25 minutes more. Cool before cutting into squares.

SHERYL TUSCH, HUDSONVILLE, MICHIGAN

SCHOOL DAY COOKIES

Because oranges were at a premium on the farm, this must have been a favorite of the Vande Bunte children! It was common to receive an orange at church for a Christmas treat when I was a little girl. We always put one in the toe of our girls' stockings at Christmas time.

1 cup solid vegetable shortening
1 cup sugar
2 cups flour
1/2 teaspoon salt
2 beaten eggs
1/4 cup orange juice
2 Tablespoons grated orange peel
1 teaspoon vanilla
1 teaspoon soda
2 cups instant oatmeal
3/4 cup chopped dates
1/2 cup nuts

Mix all ingredients. Drop on greased cookie sheet and bake at 350° until lightly browned.

SHERYL TUSCH, HUDSONVILLE, MICHIGAN

Desserts

"Everything in moderation – including moderation."

-Harvey Steiman

BANANA CAKE

This recipe came from my Mom and is one of my favorites.

2/3 cup butter, softened
1 1/2 cups of sugar
2 eggs, separated
1 cup (about 2 large) mashed bananas
4 Tablespoons sour milk
1 teaspoon soda
1 1/2 cups flour
1 teaspoon vanilla
1 cup nuts

Beat butter until fluffy. Add sugar gradually. Beat in 2 egg yolks, then mashed bananas, then the sour milk mixed with the soda. Add flour and vanilla. Beat egg whites to soft peaks and fold in with the nuts. Bake at 325° for 30 minutes.

SHERYL TUSCH, HUDSONVILLE, MICHIGAN

Editor's Note: The banana is a most curious food. Botanically speaking, it is not a fruit but rather the false berry of a gigantic herb. Its Latin name, *Musa sapientum*, means "wise person," and with their high potassium content, indeed it is wise to eat them. The peel contains dopamine and serotonin, those "feel-good" chemicals used by the brain, and the fleshy insides also stimulate mucus production in the stomach lining, perhaps why pediatricians everywhere include the banana in the recommended "BRAT" diet (Bananas, Rice, Applesauce, Toast) when little ones are suffering from tummy troubles.

Prior to the advent of refrigeration, it was difficult to ship or store bananas – they spoil quickly because they contain a high amount of polyphenoloxide, the same enzyme that makes us tan when we sit in the sun (freaky, huh?). Once refrigerated storage caught on, bananas were in high demand. Today it remains the world's most popular fruit, and for once Americans are not the biggest consumer – that honor goes to the Ugandans, who eat on average 772 pounds a year.

BAVARIAN CREAM PIE

This is the famous Bavarian Cream Pie recipe of my mother, Marian VandeBunte VanDam. She would make this every December for the VandeBunte Christmas party. I also have a wonderful picture of my daughter Jana at about 3 years of age standing up on a picnic table with pie smeared from ear to ear.

  1 cup milk
  3 egg yolks
  1/3 cup white sugar
  1/3 cup brown sugar
  pinch salt
  2 Tablespoons water
  1 packet Knox gelatin
  1 cup whipping cream
  sugar to taste
  3 egg whites, room temperature
  1 teaspoon vanilla

Stir first five ingredients constantly on stove. Watch carefully: bring to a boil, then immediately remove from heat. Add water to gelatin packet and immediately stir into mixture. Add vanilla and set aside to cool, 1-2 hours.

Whip cream and add sugar to taste. Put in refrigerator.

Whip egg whites with clean beaters until stiff. When custard has set (like "jello" is too thick, like soup is too thin), fold in whipped cream and egg whites. Spoon into baked crust (see below) and put in refrigerator for at least three hours.

Graham Cracker Crust
1 cup crushed graham crackers
1/2 cup crushed nuts
1/2 cup melted butter

Add butter to cracker crumbs and nuts and press mixture into a 9-inch pie pan. Bake in 350° oven for 10 minutes. Cool for 20 minutes. Great with Bavarian Cream Pie.

SANDRA VAN DAM ANDERSON, TUCSON, ARIZONA

BETTER THAN ANYTHING CAKE

I've seen different recipes that all fall under this title. Some combine yellow cake mix with pineapple. Now I'm sure that tastes delicious, but I'm sorry – if you're going to give a dessert this name, it had better include chocolate! This version is so good because it has the sweetness of the chocolate and cream cheese layers, combined with the salty bite of the crust. Enjoy!

1 cup flour
1 cup + 2 Tablespoons chopped nuts
1 stick butter or margarine, softened
1 8-ounce package cream cheese, softened
1 cup powdered sugar
2 cartons (8 ounces each) frozen nondairy whipped topping, thawed
3 cups milk
2 small packages instant chocolate pudding mix
2 Tablespoons shaved semi-sweet chocolate

Preheat oven to 350°. Combine flour, 1 cup of nuts and butter in a medium bowl. Press into the bottom of a greased 9" x 13" pan. Bake for 20 minutes. Cool on wire rack.

Use an electric mixer and large bowl to combine cream cheese, powdered sugar and one carton of whipped topping. Spread over cooled crust, and refrigerate. Using a clean bowl, combine milk and chocolate pudding mix. Beat three minutes at low speed until thick and glossy. Spread on cream cheese layer. Refrigerate until set. Spread remaining whipped topping over chocolate layer. Sprinkle with remaining chopped nuts and shaved chocolate.

CARAMEL APPLE CAKE

A perfect fall treat to make after visiting one of the many apple orchards in Northern Michigan!

1 1/2 cups vegetable oil
1/2 cup brown sugar
3 cups flour
1/2 teaspoon nutmeg
1/2 teaspoon salt
2 teaspoons vanilla
1 1/2 cups sugar
3 eggs
2 teaspoons cinnamon
1 teaspoon baking soda
1 cup walnuts
3 1/2 cups peeled and diced apples
Caramel Icing (see below)

In a bowl combine oil and sugars. Add eggs one at a time, beating well after each addition. Combine dry ingredients and add to batter; stir well. Fold in apples, walnuts and vanilla.

Put into an oiled 10" tube pan open or a 9 x 13" pan. Bake at 325° for 1 1/2 hours or so, until toothpick inserted in middle comes out clean. Cool and drizzle with Caramel Icing.

Caramel Icing:
1/2 cup packed brown sugar
1/3 cup heavy cream
1/4 cup butter
1 cup powdered sugar
dash salt

In the top of a double boiler heat brown sugar, cream, butter and salt until sugar is dissolved. Cool and beat in powdered sugar. Double this recipe if you like a lot of icing.

TERI MERCIER, CALGARY, ALBERTA

CHEESECAKE DESSERT

1 purchased graham cracker crust
1 (8 ounce) package cream cheese, room temperature
1/2 cup sugar
1 cup sour cream
2 teaspoons vanilla
1 9 ounce tub nondairy whipped topping, thawed
1 large can pineapple, drained
1 additional can pineapple, drained, *or* fresh berries for garnish

Beat cream cheese, sugar, sour cream and vanilla. Fold in whipped topping, thawed, and 1 can of drained pineapple and place in crust. Top with another can of drained pineapple or fresh raspberries, strawberries, or other fresh fruit.

SHERYL TUSCH, HUDSONVILLE, MICHIGAN

CHERRY COBBLER

My husband's family owns a cherry farm in Western Michigan. I don't like to make pies, so I developed this cobbler recipe. It uses the cherry mixture for a pie and a cobbler topping I found in California. I think it is much easier to make than a pie and just as delicious.

4 cups tart cherries with juice (fresh or frozen)
3-4 Tablespoons flour, more with frozen cherries
1/2 - 1 cup sugar
4 drops almond flavoring
Mix and put into a 9"x 9" baking dish.

Cobbler topping:
1 cup sugar
1 1/2 cups flour
1/2 teaspoon salt
1 1/2 teaspoon baking powder

Sift these dry ingredients together. Cut in 2/3 cup butter or margarine, and add 1 beaten egg. Mix with fork until crumbly. Sprinkle over the fruit. Bake at 375° for 35 minutes or until top is golden brown and center appears done.
GLORIA DEKLEINE, HUDSONVILLE, MICHIGAN AND SAN LUIS OBISPO, CALIFORNIA

FRESH CHERRY PIE

This recipe is a variation on the original from DeKleine Orchards in Hudsonville, Michigan. DeKleine Orchards grows cherry and chestnut trees, and offers u-pick sweet cherries and tart cherries from late June through July.

4 – 5 cups fresh sour cherries
1 1/2 cups sugar
5 Tablespoons flour or 3 Tablespoons tapioca – add more if cherries have been frozen
1/4 teaspoon almond flavoring
4 drops red food coloring
2 unbaked pie crusts

Mix cherries, sugar, flour or tapioca, almond flavoring and red food coloring together and put in pie crust. Cut second crust into lattice pieces and create lattice crust, or simply cover with second crust and cut vents for steam to escape. Bake at 415° for 25 minutes, then reduce heat to 375° and bake an additional 30 minutes. Serve warm with vanilla ice cream.

SHERYL TUSCH, HUDSONVILLE, MICHIGAN

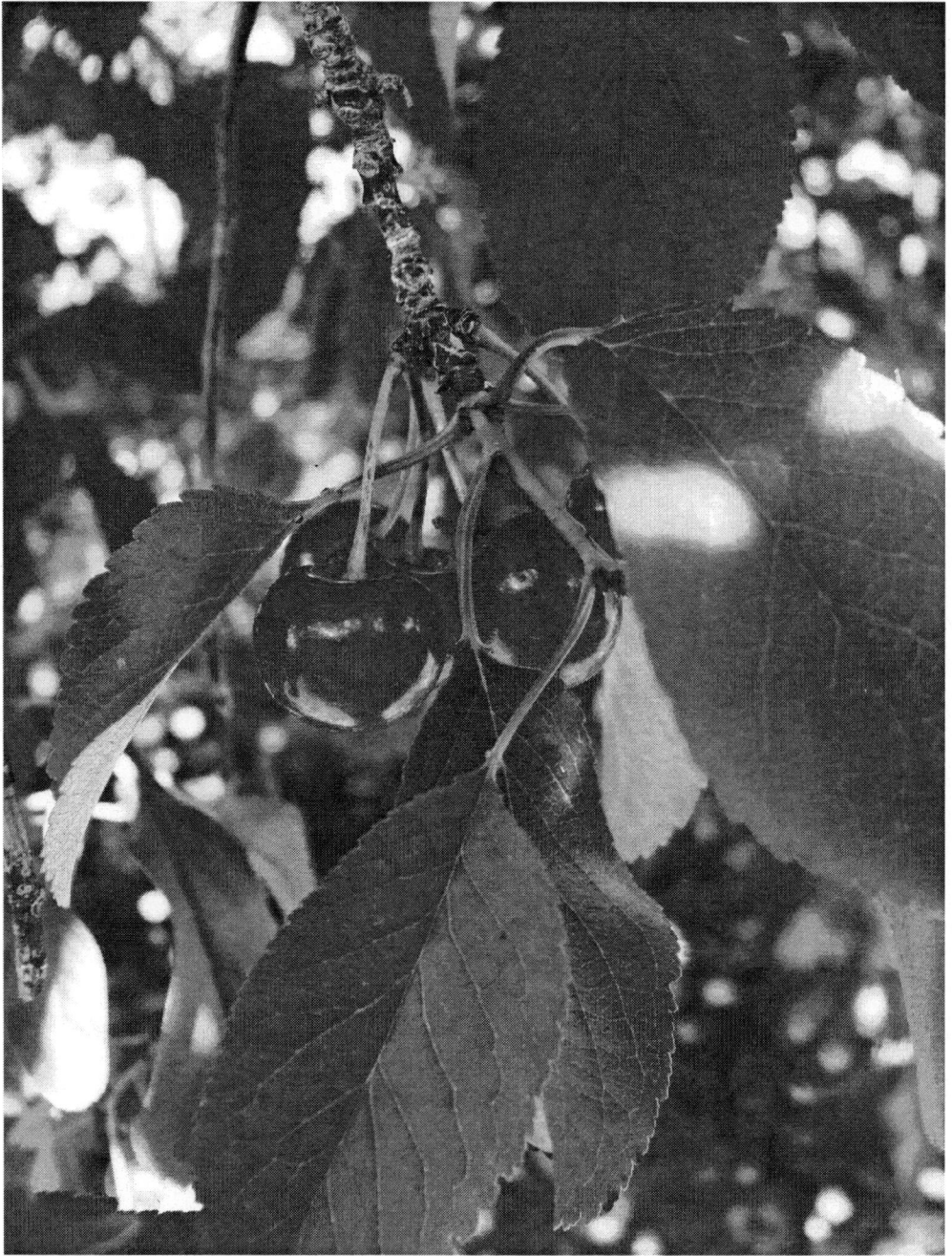

Cherries ripe for the picking at DeKleine Orchards in Hudsonville, Michigan.

CHERRY STUFF

This has been a Johnson family favorite for many years – especially at family re-unions and holiday gatherings.

Filling:
Nondairy whipped topping mix
1 (8 ounce) package cream cheese
1 1/2 cups powdered sugar
1 can cherry (or blueberry) pie filling

Crust:
1 stick butter, melted
1 package graham crackers (crushed)
2 Tablespoons powdered sugar

Make whipped topping according to package directions. Fold into cream cheese and sugar. Mix crust ingredients and press into 9 x 13 pan. Spread crust with filling, then top with cherry (or blueberry) pie filling. Refrigerate 3-4 hours.

MELISSA JOHNSON, GRAND HAVEN, MICHIGAN

CHRISTMAS YULE LOG

For many years this was my favorite Christmas cookie to make and my "secret" recipe I didn't share easily. Now I figure—share the Joy of the season—after all someone shared it with me! According to my stained recipe card it's called nut roll, but that's much too mundane for this treat!

1 pound pecan halves
1 box of graham cracker crumbs
1 pound marshmallows

1 stick (1/2 cup) of butter
1 8 ounce jar of maraschino cherries
8 ounces of coconut

In a big bowl mix the graham cracker crumbs, nuts, and coconut. In a large pan, melt butter. Add marshmallows and stir until melted. Chop cherries and add with juice to melted mixture. Combine two parts and mix thoroughly. Pour 1/4th at a time on waxed paper and roll very fast. Wrap each roll in aluminum foil and put in refrigerator. Slice into 1/2" slices when ready to serve.

SHERYL TUSCH, HUDSONVILLE, MICHIGAN

CREAM PUDDING

Because fresh eggs and milk were always available at home on the farm, Mom made this often. She often beat a couple egg whites with a bit of sugar and put this on top like whipped cream and drizzled a bit of chocolate over the top: a nice presentation from a precious, creative, frugal mom. Good memories...I still make it..

Editor's Note: "Mom" here refers to Fanny Vande Bunte, referred to as "Grandma Vande Bunte" in other recipes in this section.

4 cups milk
1 cup sugar
6 Tablespoons cornstarch
3 eggs
1 1/2 teaspoons vanilla
1/2 teaspoon salt

Heat milk to light boil. Add [mixed] beaten eggs, sugar, cornstarch, vanilla and salt. Cook till thickening. You can add coconut or bananas.

IRIS MYAARD, HUDSONVILLE, MICHIGAN

DATE CAKE

I have been making and enjoying this cake since 1970. One special day in May of 1987, I brought it on a picnic by the Rabbit River with our friends, Clark and Nancy Matthews. Myk and Gord Isenga had invited us to enjoy their woods with them and dig up as many redbud tree sprouts as we wished. The trees are still blooming on Ponca Street in the backyard and in the front yard at the Matthews' home.

1 cup dates, diced
1 1/2 cups boiling water
1 1/2 teaspoon baking soda

Mix the above ingredients and cool.

3/4 cup butter
1 cup sugar
2 eggs, beaten
1 3/4 cups flour
3/4 teaspoon baking soda
1 teaspoon salt
1 cup nuts
1 cup chocolate or caramel chips
1/3 cup sugar

Cream butter and sugar. Add eggs. Add to the date mixture. Sift flour, baking soda, and salt, and add to mixture. Put in a well-greased 9 x 13 pan. Top with nuts, chips, and sugar. Bake 45 minutes at 350°. The cake travels and freezes well.

SHERYL TUSCH, HUDSONVILLE, MICHIGAN

DATE BALLS

This is a recipe that my grandma would make for every holiday season – what sweet and delicious memories!

1/2 cup margarine
1/2 cup chopped dates
1/2 cup sugar
1 egg, beaten
1 teaspoon vanilla
2 1/2 cups crisped rice cereal
1 cup sweetened coconut

Cook first four ingredients on stove until thick. Add vanilla and cereal. Form into balls while warm, roll in coconut, and set on wax paper to cool.

MELISSA JOHNSON, GRAND HAVEN, MICHIGAN

EASY AND DELICIOUS DESSERT

This dessert is so easy to put together, and since it makes two pies, you have one to give away and one to keep for yourself. I grew up on this dessert and have made it again and again at our house. It's best made in the summer when you can get fresh Michigan strawberries, but it tastes great year-round! Make sure your butter and cream cheese are at room temperature to avoid any lumps in the bottom layer.

This recipe comes from Mavis Polavin, who published it in the 1977 Hope College Cookbook (I have replaced her cherries with strawberries for garnish). Mavis and her family attended my family's church, First Reformed Church, when I was growing up. Thank you Mavis!

    2 graham cracker crust shells
    1 (8 ounce) package of cream cheese
    1/2 cup (1 stick) butter
    1 pound powdered sugar
    6 bananas, sliced thin
    1 large can crushed pineapple, drained
    1 large container of Cool Whip
    strawberries and walnuts for garnish

Beat cream cheese, butter and sugar together until smooth. Spread over graham cracker crusts. Spread bananas over filling, and pineapple over bananas. Spread Cool Whip over pineapple. Top with strawberries and walnuts.

EASY RED VELVET CAKE

This is an easier version to serve at Christmas or any holiday where a bright red cake would be fun. It is moist and delicious. Why spend twice the time combining ingredients, when this is great. If you're in a hurry, you could even cheat and use a can of frosting, but the orange flavor gives a tasteful zing!

    1 box of yellow cake mix (18.25 ounces)
    5 eggs
    1/2 cup vegetable oil
    1 cup buttermilk
    2 Tablespoons cocoa
    2 ounces red food coloring

Combine all ingredients. Follow baking directions on the cake mix box for time to beat ingredients and how long to bake cake. DO NOT add ingredients on the cake mix.

Frosting
1 8 ounce package cream cheese, room temperature
1/2 cup (1 stick) unsalted butter, room temperture
3 1/4 cups powdered sugar, sifted
2 Tablespoons frozen orange juice concentrate, thawed
1/2 teaspoon vanilla extract

Using the electric mixer, beat cream cheese and butter in large bowl until fluffy. Beat in powdered sugar, scraping down bowl often. Beat in orange juice concentrate and vanilla. Frost. Keep cake covered and chilled. May be made a day ahead: let stand 1 hour at room temperature before serving.
SHERYL TUSCH, HUDSONVILLE, MICHIGAN

ÉCLAIR DESSERT SQUARES

This has been a favorite in our family for many years. It makes a lot of servings and carries well to a potluck if kept cold. You can also substitute chocolate flavored graham crackers for the graham crackers to "gild the lily" as it were.

2 packages of instant French vanilla pudding
3 cups of whole milk
1 9 ounce carton nondairy whipped topping, thawed
1 box of whole graham crackers
Frosting (see below)

Line a 9 x 13 pan with whole graham crackers. Mix pudding and milk. Fold in thawed whipped topping. Put half on cracker layer. Add another layer of crackers. Add the rest of the pudding. Add another layer of graham crackers. Frost and refrigerate at least 12 hours.

Frosting:
2 squares of unsweetened baking chocolate
3 Tablespoons butter or margarine
2 Tablespoons corn syrup
1 teaspoon vanilla
1 1/2 cups powdered sugar
3 Tablespoons whole milk

Melt chocolate squares and butter or margarine together. Remove from heat. Add other ingredients and mix well. Spread quickly. Add hot water if needed.

SHERYL TUSCH, HUDSONVILLE, MICHIGAN

FUDGE CHERRY CAKE

The first time I made this cake my husband had invited Ron Houle and his wife for a picnic in our backyard. I don't remember what else we ate that night, but when it was time for dessert I was very embarrassed to serve this rich chocolate cake to my Weight Watcher leader! Until they walked through the front door, I had not known who was coming for dinner!

1 box fudge cake mix
1 cup cherry pie filling
1 teaspoon almond flavoring

Prepare cake mix as directed on the box. Stir in rest of ingredients. Spread on greased jellyroll pan. Bake 30 minutes at 350°. While cake is baking, prepare frosting:

Frosting:
1 cup sugar
5 Tablespoons butter
1 /3 cup milk
1 cup chocolate chips

Mix these ingredients in a sauce pan and bring to a boil. Boil one minute. Add chocolate chips and stir until chips melt. Pour icing over cake while both are still warm. This cake freezes well.

Editor's Note: This recipe originally came from my mom's dear Aunt Henrietta, on the Yntema side of the family. Henrietta's cream puffs are the best on the planet and when she knows I'm in town she makes them. Now that's love!

SHERYL TUSCH, HUDSONVILLE, MICHIGAN

TOFFEE BAR CAKE

Baking and serving this cake always reminds me of Uncle Howard's cottage on a lovely bluff overlooking Lake Michigan. He invited our Vande Bunte family there sometimes and we loved the ride through the woods on a sandy two track up a steep hill to see the cottage through filtered sunshine. After a long trip down countless steps to the beach, playing in the water and sand, climbing back up again, we were always ravenously hungry. I brought this cake for dessert in 1969 and we have enjoyed it ever since.

2 cups brown sugar
2 cups flour
1 stick butter (1/2 cup), softened
1 egg
1 cup milk
1 teaspoon baking soda
1 teaspoon vanilla

1/2 teaspoon salt

6 to 8 chocolate-covered toffee bars

1/2 cup nuts

Cream the first three ingredients together. Set out 1 cup of this mixture. Add the rest of the ingredients (except the last two!) and mix well. Pour into greased 9 x 13 pan. Sprinkle the saved crumbs on top. Crush 6 to 8 toffee bars and sprinkle over top, then sprinkle chopped nuts. Bake 35 minutes at 350°. This cake is delicious served with whipped cream or ice cream.

SHERYL TUSCH, HUDSONVILLE, MICHIGAN

HOBO CAKE

This was my Mom's favorite cake recipe to make for my Dad. She always waited until the whole milk on the kitchen counter had turned thick and lumpy before she made the cake. She often made it for Sunday night company to serve after Waldorf salad, crackers and cheese. When we were small, Rowen and I would sometimes choose a color for the frosting. We thought she was a miracle worker! She often served a walnut half or cherry on each piece.

1 1/2 cups white sugar

1/2 cup cocoa

3 Tablespoons solid vegetable shortening

1 1/2 cups sour milk

1 1/2 teaspoons soda

1 1/2 cups flour

1 egg

Frosting (see below)

Blend ingredients and bake in 9" x 13" pan at 350° for 40 minutes. The cake will not be very tall, unless you use a 7" x 11" pan. Frost with: a walnut sized ball of butter, one cup of powdered sugar, and enough milk, orange juice, or water to moisten.

Sheryl Tusch, Hudsonville, Michigan

*Editor's Note: Growing up in West Michigan, Sunday nights usually involved a small supper since earlier in the day we would have had a "Sunday Dinner" around 1:00 or 2:00 p.m. Church services were still held every Sunday evening back then at 6:00, so we would have company over after church for a light supper or even just dessert – hence the oft-used phrase "Sunday night company." We often begged our parents not to make us go to church AGAIN (we'd been there that morning for church, then Sunday school, then choir practice in the afternoon), but when we did go we were allowed to sit in the balcony, which was a big thrill for us at the time.

MAGGIE VANDE BUNTE'S DOUGHNUTS

Maggie Vande Bunte made these doughnuts for Senator Vanden Berg from Michigan when she was his cook. My mother gave me the recipe and made them for me when I was a little girl living in Holland, Michigan. They were always a treat! We especially liked the fried donut holes!

    3 eggs
    2 cups sugar
    3 Tablespoons melted butter
    2 cups warm mashed potatoes
    3/4 cup sour milk
    1/2 teaspoon soda
    4 cups flour
    1 teaspoon salt
    1/2 teaspoon nutmeg
    4 teaspoons baking powder
    1 cup flour for rolling
    vegetable oil for frying

Beat eggs. Beat in the sugar. Add melted butter. Beat in potatoes. Add sour milk and soda. Sift flour, salt, nutmeg, and baking powder and add to batter. Roll out and cut with doughnut cutter. Fry in hot fat and drain on paper towels – take care not to crowd the pan. Shake in paper bag with sugar, powdered sugar, or cinnamon and sugar, if desired.

SHERYL TUSCH, HUDSONVILLE, MICHIGAN

MEXICAN WEDDING CAKE

This is one of my favorite recipes! I have made it for a senior band reception in 1988, teachers at Sandy Hill, Grandville Ladies Literary Society, Oak Crest Retirement Home party and for friends. It is always a reliable success!

Editor's Note: The title of this cake is a bit of a misnomer: what are traditionally considered "Mexican Wedding Cakes" are meringue-based cookies covered in powdered sugar. This recipe more closely resembles the traditional Southern American recipe for Hummingbird Cake, minus the mashed banana. Proper name or no, it's delicious!

    1 20 ounce can crushed pineapple with heavy syrup, including juice
    1 1/2 cups sugar
    2 eggs
    2 cups flour
    2 teaspoons baking soda
    1 cup chopped nuts
    1/3 teaspoon salt
    2 teaspoons vanilla

Mix all ingredients in a large bowl in order with a spoon. Pour into an ungreased 9 x 13 pan and bake at 350 for 30 – 35 minutes. Cool.

Frost with: 1 teaspoon vanilla, 1 stick soft butter, 2 cups powdered sugar, 8 oz. softened cream cheese. Mix until creamy and no lumps are left.

SHERYL TUSCH, HUDSONVILLE, MICHIGAN

ORANGE CAKE

Such an easy recipe to make! It has been a favorite of our family since I made it in the 1960s. We try not to think of all the calories, and enjoy every bite! Now our grandchildren hope I will make it when they come to visit. It travels well and freezes well, too.

1 package yellow cake mix
1 package orange gelatin, small
3/4 cup water
4 eggs
3/4 cup cooking oil

Glaze:
2 cups powdered sugar
1/2 cup orange juice

Mix cake mix and gelatin. Add water and eggs. Beat with mixer 3 minutes. Add oil and beat one minute more. Pour into greased 9 x 13 pan. Bake 35 – 40 minutes at 350°. Cool 20 minutes. Prick full of holes with a large tined fork. Mix glaze ingredients with whisk and pour over cake.

SHERYL TUSCH, HUDSONVILLE, MICHIGAN

Editor's Note: Mom's not lying when she says the grandkids hope she'll make it when they visit. All you have to say are the words "orange cake," and all six of them get the same look in their eyes. Think "winner of Publisher's Clearinghouse" meets "deer caught in the headlights." Yeah, it's that good.

RHUBARB CREAM PIE

This is a great pie to make in the early summer, when the fresh rhubarb is tender. Check out your guests first—Friends either adore or don't like rhubarb pie. Serve this special one only to those who will appreciate your efforts!

3/4 cup brown sugar
3/4 cup sugar
3 Tablespoons flour
1/2 teaspoon nutmeg
1/2 teaspoon almond extract
2 well-beaten eggs
3 cups diced fresh rhubarb
1 Tablespoon cold butter
2 purchased, unbaked pie crusts
cream and sugar

Preheat oven to 450°. Blend first five ingredients. Add eggs and beat until thick and smooth. Add rhubarb and mix. Pour into a pastry-lined 9 inch pie pan. Dot with butter. Make a lattice crust by cutting the other pie shell into 1/2 inch strips. Weave into lattice design. Brush the top with a little cream and sprinkle lightly with sugar. Bake 10 minutes at 450° then 30 minutes at 350 degrees until golden brown. Let cool before serving.

SHERYL TUSCH, HUDSONVILLE, MICHIGAN

Editor's Note: When baking at such high heats, make sure your oven is clean to avoid smoke. If you find the rim of your pie crust is getting too brown, place strips of aluminum foil around the edges.

SEVEN UP CAKE

This cake was first made for us by Grandma Tusch, Art's Mom, for a birthday party. It is wonderful served with fresh, sliced, sweetened Michigan strawberries.

  1/2 pound butter
  1/2 cup solid vegetable shortening
  3 cups sugar
  5 eggs
  3 cups flour
  3/4 cups of lemon-lime soda
  3 Tablespoons of butter and nut flavoring (or 1 1/2 Tablespoons butter flavoring, 1 Tablespoon almond flavoring)
  1 1/2 cups pecans

  Mix in order given. Bake in a greased tube pan for 1 1/2 hours at 300°.
  SHERYL TUSCH, HUDSONVILLE, MICHIGAN

STRAWBERRY PIE

Every June when I have to bring a dessert to a potluck, I consider this pie. It is best made with Michigan strawberries, on the market such a short time. I have tried other strawberry pie recipes that are more complicated, but keep returning to this one—my favorite!

  1 cup water
  1 cup sugar
  3 Tablespoons cornstarch
  3 Tablespoons strawberry-flavored gelatin
  1 quart strawberries
  a little red food coloring (optional)
  a few drops of almond flavoring (optional)

1 baked and cooled pie shell

Boil the first three ingredients until thick. Cool 10 minutes. Add gelatin and mix well. Pour over 1 quart strawberries (slice the big ones and arrange small ones, tips up, on top).

SHERYL TUSCH, HUDSONVILLE, MICHIGAN

TEXAS SHEET CAKE

This is a family favorite to take on picnics, have for a bedtime snack with a cold glass of milk, or keep in the freezer for unexpected company. This is one of very few recipes I make where I think margarine works better than butter. Go figure! Sometimes I mix and spread the frosting, sprinkling the nuts on top, instead of stirring them in.

1 cup (2 sticks) margarine
1 cup water
2 eggs
2 cups sugar
2 cups flour
1/2 teaspoon salt
4 Tablespoons cocoa
1 teaspoon baking soda
1/2 cup sour milk or buttermilk*

Frosting:
1/2 cup margarine
4 Tablespoons cocoa
6 Tablespoons milk
1 pound box powdered sugar
1 cup nuts
1 teaspoon vanilla

Bring margarine and water to a boil: set aside. In a large bowl mix remaining ingredients together, then add margarine and water mixture. Bake in a 15 x 10 jelly roll pan at 375° for 15 minutes. Cool. Add frosting according to directions below:

Frosting

Bring margarine, cocoa and milk to a boil. Add to powdered sugar, nuts, and vanilla. Stir fast by hand and *spread quickly* as it sets up fast!

*Sour milk=1tbsp. lemon juice to 1 cup milk if you don't have sour milk or buttermilk.

SHERYL TUSCH, HUDSONVILLE, MICHIGAN

Main Dishes and Casseroles

GRANDMA YNTEMA'S AFRICAN CHOW MEIN

We often had this on Saturday nights around Grandma's big table with her delicious homemade bread, baked that morning, red jello with fruit, pickles, potato chips and other treats the aunts brought. It was soul food for us all. We knew her custard and apple pies would follow! Sweet memories.

    1 pound cubed veal or lean pork
    salt and pepper
    1 medium onion, sliced
    1 cup diced celery
    1/2 cup raw rice
    1 can cream of chicken soup
    1 can cream of mushroom soup

1 can of water

Brown meat in a large skillet and season with salt and pepper. Remove meat. Brown celery and onion in same pan. Add rest of the ingredients. Place in a buttered casserole or a 9 x 13 pan and bake covered for 1 hour at 350°. Uncover and bake another 1/2 hour. You can double the recipe—use two casseroles—and then hold it all in a large crockpot if you want to serve it at a potluck or buffet.

SHERYL TUSCH, HUDSONVILLE, MICHIGAN

PEANUT BUTTER PORK CHOPS

This recipe was given to me by Marcia Schuette, one of my fourth grade students at Sandy Hill School. I still use her penciled copy, barely legible, when I make these wonderful pork chops and remember her. I have long forgotten why she gave me the recipe! We served them to our minister and his wife recently, Rich and Marge Baukema, after we noticed he attended all our Wednesday evening dinners with a jar of peanut butter in his back pocket to spread on our delicious bread at church. He liked them and he especially liked the idea of peanut butter in the recipe.

    4 large loin pork chops
    oil
    4 thin onion slices
    1/2 can of cream of mushroom soup
    1/4 cup of milk
    1/4 cup of peanut better
    1 teaspoon Worcestershire sauce
    1 teaspoon salt
    1/8 teaspoon pepper

Heat small amount of oil in large pan and brown chops on both sides. Pour off extra fat when chops are browned. Put a slice of onion on each chop. Mix soup and milk and blend well. Add peanut butter, Worcestershire sauce, and seasonings. Pour over chops. Cover skillet and cook over low heat for 45 minutes, or put in a 350° oven for the same time.

SHERYL TUSCH, HUDSONVILLE, MICHIGAN

PORK TENDERLOIN WITH MUSTARD SAUCE

This marinade is also great for other cuts of pork, as well as chicken. We like it best grilled for a perfect summer cookout!

2 1/2 - 3 pounds fresh pork tenderloin

Marinade:
1/4 cup soy sauce
1/4 cup bourbon
2 Tablespoons brown sugar

Mustard Sauce:
1/3 cup sour cream
1/3 cup mayonnaise
1 Tablespoon dry mustard
1 Tablespoon finely chopped scallions
1 1/2 teaspoons vinegar
Salt to taste

Mix together sour cream and mayonnaise, then stir in remaining ingredients.

Marinade meat in resealable plastic bag for several hours (or overnight for best flavor).

Remove from marinade and bake for 1 hour in slow oven at 325° basting frequently with marinade, or grill.

Carve on the diagonal in thin slices and serve with mustard sauce.
MELISSA JOHNSON, GRAND HAVEN, MICHIGAN

SHERYL'S GOULASH

I had been making goulash ever since our camping days, forty years ago, when it would be a quick meal to heat up the first night at the camp site. When we served it to our friends, Chuck and Sharon Porte, she asked me for my recipe. After all these years, I finally wrote it down as I made it. If you want to kick it up a notch even further, you can add Tony Chachere's Creole Seasoning to taste.

2 pounds ground beef
1 medium onion, chopped
1 cup chopped celery
1 16 ounce box elbow macaroni
8 ounces Contadina tomato sauce
1 28 ounce can chopped tomatoes
1 Heinz chili sauce
1 1/4 cup Heinz ketchup
2 teaspoon salt
1/2 teaspoon pepper
1 teaspoon basil
2 teaspoons oregano
1 1/2 teaspoons dried parsley
1 teaspoon sugar
2 teaspoons vinegar
2 teaspoons chili powder

In a large skillet, brown meat until no longer pink. Remove with slotted spoon. Brown onion and celery in same pan. Drain excess fat. Cook the macaroni according to directions on the box. Add all the ingredients and simmer 10 minutes. It is even better the next day!

SHERYL TUSCH, HUDSONVILLE, MICHIGAN

ZUCCHINI QUICHE

Mouthwatering and delicious! This has been a tradition every summer at our Holland cottage since August 1995 when Mary Malloy, a family friend, made it for us – we eat it many times a year. It's simple and everyone loves it! We've given this recipe out to many people.

2 Tablespoons butter
3 medium zucchini, washed and sliced thin (skin on or off)
1 medium onion, thinly sliced
1 teaspoon ground black pepper
8 ounces shredded mozzarella (or more if you prefer)
3 eggs
3 Tablespoons milk
3 Tablespoons sour cream
2 packages refrigerated crescent-shaped rolls
1 Tablespoon Dijon or spicy mustard
1 teaspoon dried oregano
1 teaspoon dried basil

Melt butter in large sauté pan, and sauté zucchini and onion until soft and caramelized. Sprinkle with ground pepper and set aside. In a small bowl, stir together eggs, milk and sour cream, and set aside.

Grease deep-dish pie pan or deep-dish round baking stone with non-stick cooking spray, and preheat oven to 350°. Press crescent rolls in bottom and up

sides of dish to form a crust. Spread mustard on bottom of crust, then spread
half of sautéed zucchini mixture on top. Layer half the mozzarella, sprinkle
herbs, then layer remaining zucchini and cheese. Top with egg mixture, and
bake 25 minutes or until golden brown.

SHAWN COLE, GRAND RAPIDS, MICHIGAN

Salads and Sides

*A fruit is a vegetable with looks and money. Plus, if you let fruit rot, it turns into
wine, something Brussels sprouts never do.*

~P.J. O'Rourke

ASPARAGUS WITH DIJON MUSTARD SAUCE

This reminds me of the asparagus served at Julia and Tom Beyer's wedding reception after their traditional Greek ceremony, in front of the fireplace in a lovely
East Grand Rapids home. She made a beautiful bride, however her advanced
cancer made it a bittersweet day.

   1 pound asparagus, trimmed
   1 teaspoon Dijon mustard
   1 Tablespoon red wine vinegar
   3 Tablespoons olive oil
   Freshly ground black pepper, to taste

   Boil or steam asparagus 3 to 5 minutes, until just tender.

Put rest of the ingredients in a small jar and shake to blend. Pour over asparagus and serve immediately. Serves 4. Use the sauce sparingly—the flavor is very strong!

SHERYL TUSCH, HUDSONVILLE, MICHIGAN

Editor's Note: I was one of many guests at the wedding who asked about the asparagus – it was served room temperature, drizzled with some Champagne vinaigrette. A good alternative to the above recipe, if you're out of Dijon. Memories of Tom and Julia's wedding will stay with me for a long time, not only because it was beautiful and full of joy despite the sadness of Julia's diagnosis, but because several months later, on the same day her spirit left this world, a new one arrived in the form of our precious son, Tommy.

AUNT MARIE'S SALAD

Aunt Marie brought this "secret recipe" for many years to the Yntema potlucks, before revealing the ingredients. I think she thought the idea of buttermilk would turn people off. It is creamy and light. In later years I learned any flavor of gelatin can work, but hers was always apricot.

6 ounces apricot-flavored gelatin (dry)
1 (20 ounce) crushed pineapple, drained
9 ounces Cool Whip
2 cups buttermilk

Cook the drained pineapple and gelatin until clear. Cool. Add Cool Whip and buttermilk. Refrigerate until set. Serve with a dollop of real whipped cream.

SHERYL TUSCH, HUDSONVILLE, MICHIGAN

BROCCOLI-CAULIFLOWER SALAD

1 good-sized bunch of broccoli, cut into bite-sized pieces
1 medium-sized cauliflower, but into bite-sized pieces
1 jar real bacon bits
1/4 cup finely chopped red onion
1 cup dried Michigan cherries or raisins (or a combination of the two)

Dressing:
1 cup real mayonnaise
1/4 cup sugar
2 teaspoons white vinegar

Mix the first five ingredients. Combine mayonnaise, sugar and vinegar and pour over the vegetables. Toss gently. Cover and chill for several hours or overnight before serving. You may add 1/2 cup canned pineapple tidbits and 1/2 cup chopped, pitted dates.

We like this way of adding vegetables and fruit to our diet. It makes a good addition to a buffet or can be served as a main course at lunch.

SHERYL TUSCH, HUDSONVILLE, MICHIGAN

BRAISED BROCCOLI OR BRUSSELS SPROUTS

3 cups water
12 cups broccoli florets or Brussels sprouts
1 cup whipping cream
1 Tablespoon orange juice concentrate, thawed
3/4 teaspoon salt
1/2 teaspoon pepper
1/3 cup sliced almonds or pecans, toasted

In a large pan boil water and salt. Add vegetables. Return to boiling. Cook, covered, 8 to 10 minutes or until tender. Drain. Pour into large bowl. Add cream, juice, and pepper to pan. Heat through. Spoon over vegetables. Sprinkle on nuts. Serves twelve.

SHERYL TUSCH, HUDSONVILLE, MICHIGAN

CARROT PENNIES

I first served this in 1974 at Easter time. The girls liked the shape and taste. If you are watching calories, this is a good option to brown sugar and butter on carrots. Because they are baked in the oven, you don't need to watch that the pan will boil dry!

  1 quart very thinly sliced carrots
  1/2 teaspoon dried basil leaves
  1/2 teaspoon salt
  1/4 cup water
  2 Tablespoons butter

Place carrots in a 1 1/2 quart casserole. Stir in basil, salt, and water. Dot with butter. Cover and bake 65 to 70 minutes, until fork-tender. Serves 6.

SHERYL TUSCH, HUDSONVILLE, MICHIGAN

CHRISTMAS LAYERED SALAD

When our girls were home for Christmas, this was a must serve! The red, white, and green layers are festive for a Christmas potluck or group party.

  1 package lime-flavored gelatin
  1 package lemon-flavored gelatin
  1 packages cherry-flavored gelatin

1 (20 ounces) can crushed pineapple
1/2 cup chopped celery
6 ounces cream cheese, room temperature
1/3 cup salad dressing
1 jar of cranberry orange relish

Dissolve lime gelatin in 1 1/4 cups boiling water, add pineapple (with juice) and celery. Pour in a 9 x 13 pan, chill until set. Dissolve lemon gelatin in 1 1 / 4 cups boiling water. When gelatin has cooled, add cream cheese and salad dressing. Stir until blended. Strain as you pour over green layer. Chill until set. Dissolve cherry gelatin in 1 1/4 cups boiling water, add cranberry orange relish and stir. Set until well chilled. This takes a while to make, because each layer has to set.

SHERYL TUSCH, HUDSONVILLE, MICHIGAN

CORN PUDDING

After trying many recipes for this comfort food, I always return to this very old one—my favorite.

2 Tablespoons sugar
1 1/2 Tablespoons cornstarch
1 cup whole milk
3 eggs, beaten
1 can (1 pound) cream-style corn
2 Tablespoons butter, melted
1/2 teaspoon salt
1 dash nutmeg

Mix sugar and cornstarch together. Add milk, gradually, stirring until smooth. Add eggs, corn, butter and salt. Mix well. Pour into greased 1 quart baking dish. Sprinkle with nutmeg. Put in pan of hot water. Bake at 300° for 1 3/4 hours, or until custard is set. Serves 4 to 6.

SHERYL TUSCH, HUDSONVILLE, MICHIGAN

Editor's Note: If you're nervous about carrying the pan of hot water with the casserole dish inside, you can pour in a little hot water in the pan, place the casserole inside, place it on the oven rack, then fill up with more hot water until it's about halfway up the side of the casserole.

FRENCH BUTTERED PEAS

2 packages (1 pound each) frozen peas
3 lettuce leaves, broken
1 Tablespoon sugar
1 teaspoon salt
1/2 cup water
3 Tablespoon butter

Heat peas, lettuce, sugar, salt, and water to boiling in medium-size pan. Cover and cook 10 to 15 minutes or until peas are tender. Drain. Remove lettuce and stir in butter.

SHERYL TUSCH, HUDSONVILLE, MICHIGAN

FRESH VEGETABLE CASSEROLE

3 (8 inch) zucchini
2 tomatoes
2 medium onions
3 slices whole-wheat bread
2 eggs, slightly beaten
1 teaspoon oregano or Italian seasoning

2 cups grated Cheddar or Colby cheese

Grease a 10" square microwave dish. Slice zucchini in thin rounds. Cut to-matoes and onions in thin slices. Crumble bread into bowl. Add beaten eggs, and stir to mix. Spread mixture in dish. Layer vegetables over bread mix-ture. Sprinkle with spice. Cover with waxed paper or dish cover. Bake in mi-crowave oven for 15 minutes. Rotate pan one-quarter turn every 5 minutes. Remove cover. Sprinkle with cheese. Return to microwave oven and cook just until cheese is melted. (This can be baked in a conventional oven at 350 degrees for 45 minutes, plus 5 minutes for melting cheese.)

SHERYL TUSCH, HUDSONVILLE, MICHIGAN

MANGO JICAMA SALAD

This salad is a great, cool, contrast to spicy flavored Mexican food.

2 cups julienned peeled jicama
2 cups chopped peeled mango
1/2 cup dried cranberries
2 green onions, thinly sliced
3 cups mixed salad greens

Dressing
2 Tablespoon Olive oil
2 Tablespoon orange juice
2 Tablespoon lime juice
dash salt and pepper

Shake dressing ingredients in a tight fitting jar. Place torn salad greens in a glass bowl and add the rest of the ingredients on top. This is an unusual salad, tasty, and worth the effort of time consuming chopping. Serves four.

SHERYL TUSCH, HUDSONVILLE, MICHIGAN

MARINATED VEGETABLES

4 cups assorted fresh vegetables, such as carrots, cauliflower, broccoli, summer squash, zucchini, jicama, and pea pods

1/4 cup lemon juice
1 Tablespoon sugar
1 teaspoon salt
1 teaspoon oregano leaves, fresh
1/8 teaspoon pepper

Place vegetables in a shallow baking dish or casserole. In a small bowl mix remaining ingredients. Pour over vegetables. Cover and refrigerate 6 hours or overnight, stirring occasionally. Serve on a bed of lettuce. Serves four.
SHERYL TUSCH, HUDSONVILLE, MICHIGAN

ORANGE SODA POP SALAD

This salad is always a hit. It brings back lots of memories for me. I took it to Uncle Henry's cottage in 1969, to Yntema get-togethers in the 70s, to Mom Tusch's birthday party in 2000 and made it for Tommy's baptism in 2002.

2 packages orange gelatin
2 cups boiling water
1 (12 ounce) bottle orange soda pop
1 (20 ounce) can crushed pineapple, drained
1/2 pint whipping cream (whipped)
1 cup marshmallows, cut in small pieces.

Dissolve the gelatin in water. Stir until dissolved. Add orange pop, pineapple. Cool until slightly jelled. Add whipping cream, marshmallows and mix thoroughly. Pour into 9 x 13 pan. Refrigerate to set.

SHERYL TUSCH, HUDSONVILLE, MICHIGAN

ROASTED BROCCOLI AND PECANS

1 head of broccoli, cut into florets, including stem pieces
1/4 cup olive oil
1/2 teaspoon salt
1/4 teaspoon pepper
1/4 cup pecans

Heat oven to 400 degrees. In a roasting pan, combine all the ingredients. Roast, stirring once, until tender, 20 to 25 minutes. Wonderful and easy!
SHERYL TUSCH, HUDSONVILLE, MICHIGAN

The Portable Potluck

Anyone who has ever camped in the backcountry will tell you that good food is critical to the success of any trip. An excellent meal on the trail tastes ten times as good, and seems ten times as precious, as one at home, whereas a meal of cold jerky and granola bars, while sufficient, can drop-kick even the perkiest campers' morale in a hurry. My friends and I have traditionally used our backcountry camping trips as excuses to eat like kings. It's all about the food, baby – and where permitted, it's also about the good ol' box of wine.

One memorable dinner on Michigan's North Manitou Island, just off the shore of Sleeping Bear Dunes National Lakeshore, ended with an impromptu birthday cake. I had already planned to make backpacker cheesecake, and earlier that day we had discovered a bounty of wild strawberries near our campsite. We picked enough to top the cheesecake I had made, someone found a candle, and we sang "Happy Birthday" to our good friend Tim Speck. Making the cheesecake was so simple, but it's those little indulgences that make all the difference.

Here's a dinner menu for backpackers limited to camp stoves, ziplock bags and water bottles.

EBERLE'S TRAVELING BRUSCHETTA

Our friend Bill Eberle often shared this with us so I'm going to give him the credit. A fun way to do this with a group is assembly-line style. Sit in a circle and pass the ingredients down the line in the order they are assembled. By the time the last bowl has been passed around, everyone's made their own bruschetta.

Here's a bit of trivia to share with your fellow campers while you're munching: basil was named by the Greeks, who gave it the esteemed title of *basilikos*, or King of Herbs (basileus means king; the Latin name is ocimium basilicum). It is part of the mint family, was first developed in India and is sacred to the Hindu gods Vishnu and Krishna.

At home:

Pack a baguette or similar crusty bread, one block of mozzarella, four plum tomatoes and sixteen leaves of basil, already washed and dried. Pour olive oil or herbed olive oil into a small squeezable bottle.

At camp:

Slice tomatoes and cheese. Tear or cut slices of bread, and top each with one slice of cheese, then one tomato slice. Drizzle with a little olive oil and top each piece with one leaf of basil.

BACKPACKERS' SOUTHWEST PAELLA

The first weekend in June means camping on North or South Manitou Islands. Now that we live in Calgary, we mope around the house that weekend knowing we're missing out on big fun. Thankfully, our gang still includes us by asking for recipes to share with everyone. My friend Michelle asked for a recipe for paella that could be made in camp, so I did a little research, combined different ingredients and came up with this. I hear it was a big hit!

3 Tablespoons olive oil
1 small white onion, chopped into large pieces
6 cloves of garlic, finely chopped
1 cup roasted red peppers, cut into large pieces
2 large jalapenos, seeded and diced
1 ounce sun-dried tomatoes
1 small can of sliced black olives
2 ounces dried peas (optional)
1 or 2 6-ounce cans chicken
1 or 2 6-ounce cans shrimp
4 ounces dried spicy sausage, (e.g. pepperoni) sliced (optional)
3 cups quick-cooking rice
1 1/2 Tablespoons paprika
2 bay leaves
1 Tablespoon parsley flakes
1Tablespoon oregano
1 teaspoon red pepper flakes
2 chicken boullion cubes
Salt and pepper

At home:

Prepare vegetables as indicated and place into individual plastic bags. Add herbs, spices and boullion cubes to rice and place in plastic bag. Place bags into a single larger bag and refrigerate.

At camp:

Drain olives, chicken and shrimp. Add olive oil to a large skillet and heat. Add chopped onions, garlic and jalapeños. Cook over low heat until onions are fully cooked and soft. Add six cups of water and rice-and-seasoning mixture, and tomatoes. Cover and cook over low heat for approximately five-ten minutes. Add the peas, peppers, drained olives, sausage rounds and drained chicken and shrimp. Cook five minutes longer, covered. Season to taste.

DECADENT BACKPACKER CHEESECAKE

This is the recipe for Tim Speck's birthday cake that I still hear about. I remember on the same trip poor Tim overestimated the need for flour tortillas and in an attempt to unload them, kept saying, "that'd be great as a wrap!" whether we were eating curry, gorp or oatmeal.

You can purchase the type of cheesecake mix that comes with the topping, but it adds significant weight to your pack and certainly doesn't taste homemade. A better alternative, in my opinion, is to use what's around your site. If you use wild berries, be sure you can differentiate between safe and poisonous varieties. Lacking wild berries, you could add any of the toppings mentioned below.

At home:

Mix a purchased no-bake cheesecake mix with one heaping 1/2 cup of powdered milk and place in a resealable plastic bag. In a separate bowl, mix graham cracker crumbs with sugar and melted butter, according to package directions, and place in a separate plastic bag (if you're hiking in a hot climate and are concerned about packing butter, replace butter with Butter Buds and add water in camp as needed). Refrigerate until you're ready to leave.

At camp:

Press crumb mixture into pie pan, small skillet or bowl. Add 1 1/2 cups of very cold water to cheesecake bag and mix well. Spread on top of crumbs and allow it to set. Note that the warmer the climate, the longer this will take. Top as you like with any of the following: wild berries, granola, jam, shaved chocolate, or dried fruit, slightly reconstituted in water.

PEPPERMINT FIREWORKS

This isn't so much a recipe as it is a suggestion for after-dinner refreshment and entertainment, all in one. When you're carrying everything on your back, a small item that does double duty is invaluable. Here's what you do:

Wait until it is completely dark at your campsite. Pass around some PepOMint Lifesavers and, making sure you have an audience within viewing distance, crunch one with your back teeth – with your mouth wide open. Due to a curious phenomenon known as triboluminescence, the candies will actually make sparks in your mouth. Think of it as tiny fireworks – it's a hit with the little ones, especially when they can show off for their friends!

New England and Mid-Atlantic

NEW ENGLAND CLAM CHOWDER

"Chowder breathes reassurance. It steams consolation."
-Clementine Paddleford

Chowder comes from the French *chaudron*, which was the pot used to cook the thick soup. Clam chowder most likely traveled to New England from Breton fishermen in Atlantic Canada, who would toss fish pieces in the pot to make a stew (think French bouillabaisse). Several variations of chowder now appear across the United States, but one of the originals, and still a classic, is New England (or Boston) Clam Chowder.

    6 slices bacon
    1 onion, diced
    1 stalk celery, diced
    1 large carrot, peeled and diced
    2 cups diced small white new potatoes (no need to peel)
    1-3 Tablespoons vegetable oil
    2 Tablespoons flour

1/2 cup clam juice
1 cup chicken stock or chicken broth
1 cup drained canned clams (about one large can's worth)
1 1/2 cups half-and-half
1/2 teaspoon Kosher salt
1/2 teaspoon ground black pepper
2 Tablespoons chopped fresh parsley

Chop bacon and add to a large saucepan. Fry bacon until crisp, remove pieces and reserve, draining on a plate lined with paper towel. To bacon drippings still in pan, add onion, celery, carrot and potato. Sauté on medium-high heat until vegetables are tender, adding vegetable oil if needed. Add flour and stir through vegetables for two minutes. Add clam juice, scraping up any browned bits from the bottom of the saucepan (this is known as deglazing the pan). Add chicken stock, clams, then and half-and-half, and warm through. Do not boil, but allow the chowder to simmer gently on the stove for least five minutes, or up to twenty. Serve in dishes and garnish with bacon pieces and fresh parsley.

ℰ LEMONADE

Van Yntema, my mother, often served lemonade as an alternative to the sweetened iced tea that so many of the cooks in South Jersey used as a beverage. It is a very refreshing combination of ingredients—just right!

4 lemons
2 oranges
2 cups of sugar
pinch of salt
10 glasses of cold water
large tray of ice cubes

Juice lemons and oranges and pour juice into large pitcher. Add sugar, salt, water and ice cubes.

SHERYL TUSCH, HUDSONVILLE, MICHIGAN

GALE HOCHGRAF'S LASAGNA

Back in the early 60's when we lived in Basking Ridge, New Jersey, my husband Robert and Gale's husband, Norman, commuted to work together for a time. We still hear from them at Christmas and look forward to their news. They have lived in Maine since retiring where they can indulge their passion for sailing, and Gale is seriously playing the violin. They are a little older than us and she was a much more accomplished cook than I was. Every now and then, we would dine at each other's homes and each time I tried to improve the menu and presentation when it was my turn. I remember one dinner they were invited to which featured a frosted Christmas tree cake assembled from cutout pieces of sheet cake. It looked very good in the magazine, but I had not tried it before. The first cake I forgot about and burned it up. That got me a little rattled and I left the sugar out of number two, a rumpled mass. Number three came out in one piece, but it was so fresh it crumbled when I cut it and I had to glue the whole mess together with a whopping amount of green frosting. I ran that one down to the wire and I was coming unglued by the time the front doorbell rang. "How very nice to see you again, join me in a martini?"

This recipe was originally taken down over the phone on an old business-size envelope. Several years ago in an effort to tidy up my recipe file and add my own notes, I began rewriting recipes. Bad idea. I overlooked this recipe many times when I wanted to make it, because I was looking for the old envelope. And all of the rewritten ones somehow lost the character of the old cooked-on originals. Thank goodness I quit before I got rid of any of my mother's recipes in her own handwriting.

Makes 2 – 7 1/2" x 11 3/4" pyrex dishes. Can easily be halved.

1 pound ground sirloin or roast beef
3 1/2 cups canned tomatoes
2 envelopes Spatini spaghetti sauce*
1 8 ounce can tomato sauce
1/8 teaspoon garlic powder
12 lasagna noodles
1 6-8 ounce package shredded mozzarella
1 cup cream-style cottage cheese
1/2 cup grated Parmesan cheese

Fry ground meat and drain cheese. Add tomatoes, spaghetti sauce mix, tomato sauce, garlic powder and simmer for 40 minutes. Meanwhile cook the lasagna noodles. Layer the meat, noodles, cottage cheese, mozzarella and Parmesan and repeat twice more for a total of three layers. Cover with aluminum foil and bake at 350° for 25-30 minutes. Can be put under the broiler for a few minutes to brown. Let stand for 15 minutes to firm up before cutting.

*Spatini is my favorite sauce, but I haven't been able to find it in the south. I now use McCormick Italian-style spaghetti sauce mix flavored with mushrooms or Paul Newman's jarred sauce with the addition of more garlic powder and Italian spices.

DEE TUSCH, MEDINA, TEXAS

MARYLAND CRABS

Shortly after my husband Adam graduated from college, he moved to Maryland to work for an airline company. He lived with his dear Grandma, Ruth Fendlay, who lived in the small town of Cape St. Clair, just outside Annapolis. I moved out to Silver Spring, Maryland shortly afterward, and on weekends, Adam and I would go down to the water, loaded with nothing but a net, some string and frozen chicken necks, and come back to her house with a basket full of Maryland Blue Crabs. I'll never forget the image of this tiny woman holding down the lid on a huge pot of crabs that clicked their claws at the top while they boiled. It was a real eye-opener for someone who was used to getting her seafood from a nice, neatly wrapped grocery store package.

Eating crabs in Maryland is a true art form, and one that lends itself well to large gatherings. Everyone sits down at a table with a section of newspaper and a hammer in front of them, and then a huge pile of cooked crabs, sprinkled generously with Old Bay Seasoning, is dumped in the middle. As you work through each crab, you fold the paper over on the shells and start fresh on a new page. Getting to the meat is an art form, and provides entertainment as well as nourishment! If you're outside of Maryland, unfortunately, it's just not the same. So lacking such a geographic advantage, I find the taste can at least somewhat be recreated in crab dip, which is also very popular in Maryland.

MARYLAND CRAB DIP

Editor's Note: The best crab dip we ever tasted was at a humble dockside bar in Annapolis called Davis' Pub. Adam and I would join our friends Tom and Dawn for a few beers and order the crab dip every time. Maryland Crab Dip always reminds me of Annapolis, a city full of history and tradition with cobblestone streets running through downtown, past the Naval Academy, and down to the waterfront. If you ever get a chance to visit Maryland, make sure to eat a pile of crabs and load up on crab dip. Whether you're in Maryland or not, Mom's hot crab dip is a sure hit!

Davis Pub, in Annapolis, Maryland.

This has been a traditional dip for special occasions in our family for many years—an annual request for Christmas hors d'oeuvres. My sister Lisa asked to have it for her college graduation—her only request.

3 (8 ounce) packages of cream cheese
2 (7 1/2 ounce) can of all white crab meat, drained, flaked
1 clove garlic, crushed
1/2 cup real mayonnaise
2 teaspoons dry mustard
2 teaspoons confectioners' sugar
seasoned salt to taste
1/4 cup white wine

Combine all ingredients. Heat in a chaffing dish or microwave. Serve with Triscuits. It may be frozen and reheated.

SHERYL TUSCH, HUDSONVILLE, MICHIGAN

Southeast and Low Country

"NOTHING REKINDLES MY SPIRITS, GIVES COMFORT TO MY HEART AND MIND, MORE THAN A VISIT TO MISSISSIPPI.... AND TO BE REGALED AS I OFTEN HAVE BEEN, WITH A PLATTER OF FRIED CHICKEN, FIELD PEAS, COLLARD GREENS, FRESH CORN ON THE COB, SLICED TOMATOES WITH FRENCH DRESSING.... AND TO TOP IT ALL OFF WITH A WEDGE OF FRESHLY BAKED PECAN PIE."

-Craig Claiborne

BRUNSWICK STEW

While living in North Carolina for many years I was invited to several "block parties" usually thrown between Halloween and Thanksgiving. These block parties always consisted of a pig roast (cooking a pig on a spit is a bit of an art form in North Carolina) and usually a big pot of Brunswick stew.

Brunswick stew was traditionally a harvest-time celebration for a farmer and his neighbors. A stew was a good way to use up the last vegetables from a summer garden and a way of celebrating the tobacco harvest and providing a treat for the hardworking neighbors, friends and hands who had helped a farmer make his crop.

Here's a recipe for a 25-gallon pot, make sure to invite the neighbors for this one:

By first light, have water boiling in the pot. Add 2 cleaned squirrels, 8 pounds of pork, 8 pounds of beef and 7 fresh frying chickens (never frozen), 2 pounds of onion and 2 pods, red cayenne pepper. Cook at a roiling boil until mid-morning. Add a gallon of baby butter beans. Add water as necessary. Keep at a boil. Pick bones out as meat settles. Add 3 Tablespoons salt and pepper every time you add ingredients. Around 1 o'clock, add 10 pounds of potatoes, peeled and quartered. Around 3 o'clock, scoop out the red peppers and add 8 quarts of tomatoes, skinned and seeded. An hour later, 30 minutes before serving time, add 120 ears of corn, cut off the cob and frozen. Just before serving, add 1 pound butter, 1 cup vinegar, 1 cup sugar and a small bottle of Heinz ketchup. Cook for 15 minutes and serve. Should be ready around 6 o'clock.

JERRY BRONKEMA, ADA, MICHIGAN

Editor's Note: Before you scoff at the notion of dining on squirrel, take note: Thomas Jefferson, the gentleman farmer/statesman, believed it an essential ingredient to any Brunswick stew. This recipe is the precursor to Kentucky burgoo, a similar stew made in similar quantities, and often served at community barbeques. In 1932 a horse named Burgoo King won the Kentucky Derby.

BETTY BETTS' STINK CHEESE ITALIAN SALAD

I met Betty Betts back in the early 80's when I worked at Margie Spiller's Knit Shop in Baton Rouge. Betty was a native of Baton Rouge as were most of the other women who worked there and they all gave me great insight into the town and introduced me to the delights of needlepoint and bargello. The fifteen years we spent in Baton Rouge allowed us to travel the Pelican State, sampling the great food and music of the bayou country, visiting the great plantations along River Road and getting caught up in the ridiculous escapades of Governor Edwards, famous for his gambling and womanizing. Once as he stumbled on his way to the podium at a fundraiser, he addressed the crowd with, "Oops, must have tripped on my silver zipper." I also worked in a picture frame shop, and when Margie's closed another needlework shop. We sold our house in town and built a new one in Greenwell Springs and I finally went to college at LSU in my 40's. I had to take remedial math and for the first time, I got some understanding of algebra. Not only did we see Louisiana, but we made forays into the hills of Mississippi and the lakes of Arkansas and Alabama. Probably, the most referred to cookbooks of Baton Rouge by its cooks are *River Roads I* and *II* published by the Junior League. These are the kind of cookbooks in any city or town that reflect what the local ladies consider are their regional specialties. Betty's recipe follows.

1 cup chopped onion
1 cup chopped celery
1 cup chopped green peppers
1 5-ounce jar green olives, chopped
1 teaspoon Worchestershire sauce
3/4 cup olive oil
1 teaspoon salt
1/4- 1/2 teaspoon each: oregano, thyme, marjoram and savory (optional)
1 6-ounce can black olives chopped
2 cans anchovy fillets in oil, with capers
2 jars marinated artichoke in oil, chopped
1-2 teaspoons capers plus 1/2 teaspoon caper juice
8-10 cloves of garlic, or use powder
Juice of 3 lemons (1/2 cup)
1/2 teaspoon pepper
salad greens
fresh parsley
grated Romano

Mix all ingredients and marinate for four days in the refrigerator. Note: it may be made one day ahead and more oil may be added to make more liquid if desired. Toss with fresh greens and parsley. Add grated Romano (Betty's stink cheese) after it's tossed so it sticks to the greens. This recipe serves 20 and can easily be halved or quartered.

DEE TUSCH, MEDINA, TEXAS

CREOLE JAMBALAYA

This is one of those recipes I've made so often that I no longer use a recipe, and every time it comes out a little different. My motivation for making it so often, like every other mom, is that my kids love it, and I can sneak in the vegetables without them noticing. I usually use a spicy organic chicken sausage that I can buy at my local farmers' market, and Creole Jambalaya is usually made with andouille, but any sausage will do.

Creole Jambalaya is essentially the New World version of the Spanish paella, with tomatoes replacing the saffron, which was hard to come by when the dish was developed. Cajun jambalaya is another dish entirely, and because it does not include tomatoes, it is sometimes referred to "brown jambalaya."

2 12-inch sausages
1 onion, diced
1 green pepper, diced
2 stalks celery, diced
4 garlic cloves, minced
1 1/2 cups rice
1 cup chicken stock or water
1 large can diced tomatoes
1 1/2 Tablespoons Creole seasoning *or* 1 teaspoon each thyme, oregano, basil and 2 teaspoons paprika
1/8 teaspoon cayenne pepper (or more to taste)
1 pound shrimp, peeled and deveined
salt and pepper to taste

Slice sausages or squeeze out of casings and cook in large sauté pan. When about halfway cooked, add onion, green pepper, celery and garlic and sauté.

Depending on the type of sausage used, you may need to add a little vegetable or olive oil to keep the pan from drying out. Stir in rice, then add stock, tomatoes and seasonings. Bring to a boil, then cover and cook on low. When rice is almost cooked, add shrimp and stir through until cooked. Add salt and pepper to taste.

GEE'S JAMBALAYA

This recipe comes from a friend of my Dad's whose daughter Gee lives in Baton Rouge, Louisiana. You'll notice that hers and mine both include onion, celery, and green pepper – together these are known as the "holy trinity," and they are the Louisiana equivalent of the French *mirepoix*, which is a combination of chopped onion, celery and carrot.

2 pounds smoked sausage, sliced
2 pounds cooked boneless chicken – thighs or breast
1 pound deveined and peeled shrimp (optional)
2 pounds of cooked rice
1 medium to large chopped onion
1 medium to large chopped green pepper
1 medium to large red pepper
2 cloves of garlic
1/2-1 cup chopped celery (optional)
1 cup of chopped green onions
1/2 cup vegetable oil
1/2 to 1 cup of all purpose flour
3-6 cups of water
garlic powder and onion powder

Pour vegetable oil and flour in a pot to make a "roux" on medium heat until your roux is exactly the way you like it, thick or thin. After the roux is browned, add more water with all of your vegetables and bring to a medium-high boil for about 5-7 minutes. Then add all meats to cook for about 10 minutes on medium. Add rice and garlic and onion powder and any additional seasonings of your liking then cook for about 10 more minutes, constantly stirring. Cover and turn off heat and let sit for about 5 minutes. Stir, fluff, and serve.

GERALYN COLEMAN, BATON ROUGE, LOUISIANA

KING CAKE

Last year we had a Mardi Gras party with some neighbors and I baked a King Cake – since the kids got to search their piece for the missing plastic baby (I'll explain), it was a big hit – the baked version of a piñata, if you will.

King Cake is a New Orleans tradition dating back to the 18th century. It is served during Carnival season, from Epiphany to Mardi Gras, and decorated with the Mardi Gras colors of purple, yellow and green. It comes out of the western Christian tradition of Epiphany, the day when the three kings, or magi, visited the baby Jesus (hence the name King Cake). A small plastic baby, representing baby Jesus, is hidden in the cake, and the person who finds it gets to keep it – then it's their turn to bake the cake next year.

If you have little ones participating in this, please make sure your baby is large enough to not be a choking hazard – or remember where you put it, and carefully observe the person who receives that slice!

Cream cheese is not usually included in a King Cake, but the sweet creaminess lends itself well to this dessert, which more closely resembles cinnamon rolls than traditional "cakes." Don't let the length of this recipe intimidate you – it's really not that hard.

Dough:
1 cup milk

1/4 cup butter

2 (.25 ounce) packages active dry yeast

2/3 cup warm water

1/2 cup white sugar

2 eggs

1 1/2 teaspoons salt

1/2 teaspoon freshly grated nutmeg

5 1/2 cups all-purpose flour

vegetable oil

Filling:

8 ounces cream cheese, softened

1/4 cup powdered sugar

1 Tablespoon ground cinnamon

2/3 cup chopped pecans

1/2 cup raisins

Icing:

1 cup confectioners' sugar

2-3 Tablespoons water

Yellow, green, and purple sugar sprinkles

One small plastic baby (these can actually be found among cake-decorating supplies)

Scald milk, remove from heat and stir in 1/4 cup of butter. Allow mixture to cool to room temperature. In a large bowl, dissolve yeast in the warm water with 1 tablespoon of the white sugar. Let stand until foamy, about 10 minutes.

Mix yeast mixture with cooled milk mixture, then whisk in the eggs. Stir in the remaining white sugar, salt and nutmeg. Beat the flour into the milk/egg mixture 1 cup at a time. When the dough begins to form a ball, turn it out onto a lightly floured surface and knead until smooth and elastic, about 8 to 10 minutes. (Depending on where you live, you may not need all 5 1/2 cups of flour.)

Rub oil all over dough, place in a large bowl and cover with a clean, damp cloth. Let dough rise in a warm place until doubled in volume, about 2 hours. Punch down and divide dough in half.

Preheat oven to 375°, and grease a large cookie sheet. Mix filling ingredients together.

Roll dough halves out into large rectangles (approximately 10x16 inches or so). Spoon the filling evenly over the dough and roll up each half tightly, beginning at the wide side. Bend each roll slightly in the middle, and bring the ends of each roll together to form an oval shaped ring. Place on the prepared cookie sheet. With kitchen shears make cuts 1/3 of the way through the ring on the outer edge at 1 inch intervals. Let rise in a warm spot until doubled in size, about 45 minutes.

Bake in preheated oven for 30 minutes. As soon as the cake is out, push the doll into it (I usually "mark" it with a dent on the side of the cake). Frost while warm with the confectioners' sugar blended with 1 to 2 tablespoons of water, and add sprinkles.

Texas

Years ago Texas came up with the slogan "Don't mess with Texas" as an anti-pollution campaign. The phrase quickly caught on, and still shows up on tourist wares like t-shirts and shot glasses, as an embodiment of the Texas spirit. Texans are very proud of their state: it was, after all, the only state to successfully fight for its independence. Speaking of its independent spirit, the word *maverick*, which has come to mean a person who lives by his or her own rules, comes from Samuel Augustus Maverick, a land baron in Texas who refused to brand his cattle: to cowboys, the word came to mean any unbranded animal, because of the assumption that they were "Mavericks".

Texas is so big (everything's bigger in Texas, you know) that in terms of food the state has a regionalism all its own. Barbeque and Tex-Mex food are two obvious segments of Texas cuisine, but there are also pockets of German and Czech culture, and east Texas is so close to Louisiana its cuisine is closer to that of the Southeast and Gulf Coast, with crawfish boils, po' boys and gumbo. Now I've had my share of po' boys in Baton Rouge and New Orleans, thanks to visits to my Uncle Bob and Aunt Dee Tusch, but one of the best I ever had was at a restaurant in Galveston, Texas. Galveston is a small Gulf Coast town, but it is famous for its port and for a monstrous hurricane that roared through in 1900, flooding the city and inspiring the folk song "Wasn't That a Mighty Storm," recorded later by Nanci Griffith. It still remains the deadliest natural disaster in U.S. history (including Hurricane Katrina).

Galveston, Texas is also the site of the original Juneteenth, the holiday that celebrates emancipation from slavery in the United States. Although the Emancipation Proclamation took effect on January 1, 1863, it was on June 19, 1865, that Union troops arrived in Galveston to enforce the emancipation of slaves in Texas.

EASY PO' BOYS

The origin of the term *po' boy* is up for debate, but generally speaking it is a sandwich found along the Gulf Coast, originating in New Orleans, that features shrimp, fish, crawfish, roast beef, or oysters. Here's a recipe for po' boys that is very easy, very quick, and very popular with the kids.

4 good-quality white hoagie buns, sliced, or 1 large baguette, cut into sandwich portions
4-6 frozen breaded fish fillets
1/4 cup minced red onion
1/2 cup mayonnaise
2 cups coarsely chopped romaine lettuce

Bake fish fillets according to package directions. Meanwhile, mix onion and mayonnaise in medium bowl. Toss with lettuce. When fish is almost done, toast buns. To assemble, place 1-2 fish fillets, depending on size, on each bottom slice of the hoagie buns. Top each with lettuce mixture, and cover the sandwiches with top slices of the buns.

MARY ALICE BLACK'S LAYERED SALAD

I got the following recipe years ago from Mary Alice Black of Kingwood, Texas, a fellow member of our local segment of the Houston Embroiderer's Guild. Mary Alice hosted our Christmas party one year and it was especially nice. Her tree and decorations were lovely, but what made the event so memorable, to me, was the table centerpiece and her wonderful collection of Mexican crèche scenes displayed on bookshelves in the living room. Mary Alice was brought up in the Rio Grande Valley and had a great love and appreciation for the cross-cultural exchange between the U.S. and Mexico. A prickly pear cactus "tree" was in a prominent place on the buffet table. Made of overlapping *napalitos*, or prickly pear pads, and ornaments of small red peppers it made a colorful and charming centerpiece for a couple of her crèches and our potluck contributions. Her layered salad fit right in with the colors of the season and I made it a point to ask for the recipe before I left.

If possible use a straight-sided glass salad bowl (I use my footed trifle bowl).

1st layer:shredded romaine or head lettuce
2nd layer:1/2 pound shredded spinach
3rd layer:grape tomatoes (Dee's addition)
4th layer:one bunch green onions, chopped fine
5th layer:1 pound bacon, fried and crumbled (or Bac-Os)
6th layer:10 boiled eggs, chopped
7th layer:1 box frozen green peas, may be cooked or left raw

Make one batch of Hidden Valley Original Dressing, using the low fat directions on the package, and spread on top of salad to all edges. I always make it the night before and refrigerate it covered with plastic wrap. It's very simple, pretty and delicious. I have taken it to Friends of the Library luncheons, Stitchery meetings and I'll be taking it again to this year's Medina Garden Club salad luncheon as it's always popular. Just provide long-handled salad servers to get to the bottom of the bowl.

DEE TUSCH, MEDINA, TEXAS

CRAB QUICHE APPETIZERS

The following was inspired by a crab quiche recipe I saw years ago: I modified it to form these mini-quiche appetizers. To speed up the job, you can use a wooden "shell" tool available through food specialty stores and catalogs. One friend who requested the recipe eschewed the easy biscuit method and said she planned to use homemade pastry. I'm sure they were delicious and now that I have discovered the "tool", I may just possibly try it myself.

3 cans of flaky refrigerated biscuits (10 per can)
1/2 cup mayonnaise
2 Tablespoons cup all-purpose flour
2 eggs, beaten
1/2 cup milk
6 ounces canned crabmeat, drained
1/2 pound shredded Swiss cheese
1/3 cup finely chopped green onion

Heat oven to 375°. Cut each biscuit in half and roll into balls. Place the balls into Teflon-coated or sprayed mini muffin pans and press with thumbs to make shells. Combine mayonnaise, flour, eggs, milk; mix thoroughly. Stir in crabmeat, cheese and onion. Spoon into shells and bake for about 18 minutes. Makes approximately 60. They can be made ahead and frozen. Thaw and reheat on a cookie sheet until hot enough to serve.

Dee Tusch, Medina, Texas

PECAN TARTS

Here in Texas, west of Houston, there are many old native pecan trees in the Weston Lakes subdivision. We have three uprights and one that blew down and still bears nuts in its supine position besides providing a leafy green screen in summer. The trees have on-and-off bearing years, but there's usually at least one that produces nuts for us and the squirrels. The nuts are delicious, but small and it takes time and effort to extract the meats – which makes my little tarts especially appreciated.

This is an old recipe I first made on December 10, 1986. I have dated a lot of my favorite recipes, and I add a new date for changes or updates with new products.

Dough:
1/2 cup margarine or butter
1/2 cup sugar
2 egg yolks
1 teaspoon almond extract
2 cups flour

Filling:
1/2 cup margarine or butter
1/3 cup dark corn syrup
1 cup confectioner's sugar
1 cup chopped pecans
48 pecan halves

Cream butter or margarine and sugar. Add egg yolks, almond extract and flour. Divide dough into four quarters (12 balls), then divide each quarter in half (6 balls), and halve these sections (3 balls). Divide each into three pieces and place them in mini muffin pans.

Using your fingers or wooden tool, press the balls to create shells. Bake at 400° 8-10 minutes. If you only have a couple of muffin pans, remove shells to a cookie sheet. Make the rest of the shells and add to cookie sheet. FILLING: Bring butter or margarine, corn syrup and sugar to boil. Stir in chopped pecans and spoon into shells. Top with pecan halves. Bake at 350° for 5 minutes. Makes approximately 4 dozen tarts. I always place the shells on a round cookie sheet to fill and bake them all at once. Everyone loves these tarts and they are really easy to make with the wooden tool in assembly-line mode. Folks are sure I spent ages on making the crusts and I used to. Thumbs just don't cut it. I was just lacking the right tool for the job.

Dee Tusch, Medina, Texas

FAYE NORMAND'S CHICKEN, BLACK BEAN AND RICE CASSEROLE

I met Faye at a Forest Cove Garden Club meeting several years ago when we lived in Humble, Texas. Faye grew up in New Roads, Louisiana, is a great cook, makes beautiful cakes and even had her own catering business for a while. She and I were always involved in decorating and sometimes riding on the garden club float in the subdivision's Fourth of July parade. She was also my great biking buddy and helped me get out of the house and on the trails as I worked through the aftermath of quitting smoking. The following recipe is one of my favorites and it's popular with friends as well. In fact I took it to a Stitchery luncheon and saw another one on the counter. It belonged to a friend I had shared the recipe with. My husband Robert calls it the purple casserole, since the black beans do give it a faint tinge of purple color.

Marinade:
1/3 cup lime juice
2 1/2 Tablespoons olive oil
1/4 teaspoon ground black pepper
1/2 teaspoon garlic powder

1/2 teaspoon salt

3/4 pound boneless, skinless chicken breast

2 cups cooked rice

1 15 ounce can black beans, undrained

1/2 cup finely chopped cilantro

1/2 teaspoon onion powder

1/2 teaspoon chili powder

1/2 teaspoon ground cumin

1/2 teaspoon garlic powder

1/2 teaspoon salt

Whisk first five ingredients together in a medium bowl. Cut chicken into bite-size pieces, add to marinade, cover and refrigerate for 2 hours (if in a hurry, 15 minutes will work).

In a casserole dish combine remaining ingredients. Set aside.

With a slotted spoon, remove the chicken from the marinade and cook it in a skillet over medium heat until the juices run clear. Stir into rice mixture. Cover and bake around 40 minutes at 350° or until heated through. Makes approximately 4 1/2 cups.

DEE TUSCH, MEDINA, TEXAS

SIDENOTE: Rice combined with beans or other legumes is a dish served world-wide as an easy and economical source of protein and carbohydrates. In Nepal, for example, families cook Daal Bhat (see Nepal Section): in Cuba, black beans and rice is ubiquitous and carries the name of *moros y cristianos* – Moors and Christians (see Caribbean section).

Western States

BOLITAS DE QUESO CALIENTE

These are so yummy, they'll disappear quickly. I don't have a deep fryer, but do manage to cook these by just doing a half dozen or so at a time, and turning them in hot oil in my electric fry pan as they cook.

2 cups grated Gruyère cheese
6 walnuts, finely chopped
3 Tablespoons flour
1/2 teaspoon paprika
2 egg whites
1/2 teaspoon hot sauce
1 Tablespoon dry sherry
1 cup fine dry breadcrumbs
cooking oil

Combine cheese, walnuts, flour and paprika. Beat egg whites until very stiff; add hot sauce and sherry. Fold into cheese mixture.

Form into tiny balls, roll in bread crumbs and fry in deep, hot cooking oil until golden – be careful not to crowd the pan as you go. Remove to paper toweling; serve hot. Makes 24.

LISA MALONEY, BOULDER, COLORADO

BOULDER STEW

We love the crock pot!!! Every time I use it, I think, "Now why don't I use this more often???" Here's the perfect example of a delicious stew that you can whip up together in the morning (or even prep veggies and meat the night before), then just let that baby simmer all day. Perfect for a day when you've got better things to do (like ski, snowshoe, or just be gone for the day) than stay around the house. Smells divine, and tastes like the Old West! A simple cornbread or corn chips go well here, and haul out all your salsas and hot sauces to pass around. Freezes well, too!

3 pounds beef stew meat, cut in 1/2" cubes
2 Tablespoons olive oil
3 bay leaves
1 Tablespoon Kosher salt
2 teaspoons ground black pepper
2 Tablespoons sugar
2 Tablespoons dried parsley flakes
1 10-ounce can beef broth
2 bunches green onions, chopped
2 celery stalks, chopped
1 14-ounce can diced tomatoes
3 medium potatoes, cubed
3 carrots, sliced
1 cup red wine or one bottle dark beer
8 cloves garlic, minced
1 15-ounce can chili beans

1 1/2 cups sliced mushrooms
chili powder to taste

Place all ingredients in a 5-quart crock pot and pour water over all to fill the container. Cover and cook 8-10 hours on low or medium. If cooked on the stove, cook 6-8 hours on low heat, then 1 hour on medium heat before serving.

Lisa Maloney, Boulder, Colorado

D-9 (CHEESY POTATO CASSEROLE)

This version of the classic "cheesy potatoes" recipe is so named after the apartment building of our very dear friends, Paul and Julia who lived in Building D-9 of the University of Colorado – Boulder family housing complex. Lionel and I were in the building next door, and shared many a meal that included this casserole. At the time their two boys were seemingly always hungry, and this definitely was a hit.

1/2 stick (1/4 cup) butter
1 small onion, chopped
1 teaspoon crushed garlic
10 ounces sour cream
10 ounces shredded sharp cheddar cheese
1 can ubiquitous cream of mushroom soup
2 pounds frozen shredded hashbrowns
1 cup topping (Total cereal, crushed crackers, etc...)

In a large stockpot, melt the butter. Sauté the onion and garlic until soft. Add the sour cream and soup; mix well. Stir in the cheese until melted, then add the frozen hashbrowns; stir to coat.

Pour mixture into a 9 x 13 pan and sprinkle with your choice of topping. Bake at 350° for 45-60 minutes.

CINDY LOZA, MARION, IOWA

EASY WHITE CHILI FOR A CROWD

White Chili can be found just about anywhere across America, but when I make it I'm always reminded of my sister Lisa, who first gave me a recipe for it. Hers is just as good, but I've sliced off a couple steps in the interest of time, using rotisserie chicken from the deli in place of cooking my own. This makes a big ol' batch, so halve the recipe if you like. Feel free to adjust the chiles and spices to your own taste.

1 rotisserie chicken
2 Tablespoons olive oil
1 large onion, chopped
4 cloves garlic, minced
8 cups chicken stock
2 cups water
4 15-ounce cans white beans (I use a combination of white kidney beans, navy beans chickpeas and black-eyed peas), drained but not rinsed!
2 small cans diced green chiles
1 Tablespoon Kosher salt
1 Tablespoon ground cumin
1 Tablespoon dried oregano leaves
2 teaspoons ground black pepper
sour cream (optional)
salsa (optional)
shredded Monterey Jack cheese (optional)

Pull meat from rotisserie chicken while it's still warm (just easier that way). Set aside or refrigerate if not using right away. In large stockpot, heat olive oil then sauté onion until onion has softened. Add minced garlic and sauté one minute more. Add remaining ingredients and heat through. Serve with sour cream, salsa and shredded Monterey Jack cheese on the side.

FAVORITE PUNCH

Editor's Note: my cousin Karleen Holm has her feet in three different states: California, Colorado, and Michigan. Even though she grew up in California, her family always came back to Michigan during the summer. Like many Yntema and Vande Bunte cousins, her travels have taken her elsewhere but she keeps in touch with the rest of us, particularly when it's cherry-picking time at her family's cherry farm, DeKleine Orchards in Hudsonville, Michigan.

1 (1/2 gallon) container raspberry sherbet, softened
1 2 liter bottle of ginger ale
1 large can orange juice
1 large can pineapple juice
1 large can peaches - puree with juice and add.

Mix all together and serve.
KARLEEN HOLM, CASTLE ROCK, COLORADO

TORTILLA SOUP

Easy, delicious and great to serve on a cold day!

2 chicken breasts, cooked and diced
1 15-ounce can chicken broth
2 cups water
1 teaspoon chili powder
1 cup salsa

1 1/2 cups corn

Toppings (see below)

Mix all in a crock pot or on the stove till good and warm. Top with sour cream, cilantro, Monterey Jack cheese and tortilla chips.

KARLEEN HOLM, CASTLE ROCK, COLORADO

SOUTH AMERICA

Chile and Argentina are producing award-winning wines, Brazilian churrascurias are taking the U.S. by storm, and Lima was recently named the "Gastronomic Capital of the Americas" at the International Summit of Gastronomy in Madrid. It is exciting to see South American cuisines becoming more popular worldwide. Peru in particular is a warehouse of genetic variety when it comes to New World ingredients: it boasts 35 varieties of corn and over 2,000 varieties of sweet potato. Its historic openness to new cultural influences, particularly African, Moorish, Chinese and Spanish, its incredible diversity in topography, and recognition of pre-Columbian cuisines create a vibrant modern Peruvian cuisine. For more on South America, see the "Cowboy Cuisine" section under the chapter on Canada.

CHIMICHURRI

Chimichurri is gaining popularity in steakhouses across North America. With the piquant combination of fresh herbs, garlic, and olive oil, it's almost a cross between salsa verde and pesto. I've seen several variations on the theme, with ingredients like cilantro, lime, tomatoes and onions in the mix, but the essentials are fresh parsley, olive oil and lemon.

There are competing stories on how chimichurri got its name, but it is essentially an Argentinian creation, designed to complement grilled meat, or *asado*. Serve chimichurri with grilled steaks, burgers, chicken, fish, or even spoon a little on scrambled eggs.

> 1 lemon
> 2 cups chopped fresh parsley
> 2 cloves garlic, minced
> 1 Tablespoon onion, minced
> 3/4 cup olive oil
> 1/4 cup red wine vinegar
> salt and pepper to taste

Grate the zest of the lemon and place in a blender or food processor. Juice the lemon, and add the juice and remaining ingredients to the blender. Pulse just a few times to blend, keeping the parsley leaves still visible (think textured sauce, not smoothie). Serve as an accompaniment to grilled meat or fish.

PAPA RELLENA (STUFFED POTATO)

Quite a complicated recipe, but these are sooo good. Our friends from International family housing at CU-Boulder made these any time they had a party and they always disappeared quickly. Jenny and Koki are from Peru, and there was always something yummy cooking in their kitchen.

2 1/2 pounds white potatoes
4 eggs (3 hard boiled, one fresh)
6 Tablespoons vegetable oil, separated
1 cup chopped onion
1 clove garlic, minced
1 pound ground beef
1/2 cup peeled, seeded, chopped tomatoes
1 teaspoon paprika
6 black olives
1 teaspoon chopped parsley
1 teaspoon chopped fresh cilantro
1/4 cup raisins
salt, pepper and paprika
Onion Relish (see below)

Wash the potatoes. Cook in boiling salted water until soft. Remove, and peel. Smash the cooked potatoes with a fork, and let them cool down. Knead in the fresh egg and 1/2 teaspoon each salt and pepper until the mixture gets soft. Set this aside.

Pour 2 Tablespoons oil into skillet. Brown the onion and then add the garlic. Add the ground beef and chopped tomato, and cook this mixture for 5 minutes, or until the meat is cooked through. Add the paprika, olives, parsley, cilantro, hard boiled eggs (chopped), and raisins. Season with salt, pepper, and paprika.

Flour your hands, take about 1/2 cup of the "dough" and put it in your palm. Flatten it. In its center, put a tablespoon of stuffing and fold to envelop it, pressing to close well, giving it an oval shape. Flour it. Repeat with remaining dough and stuffing.

Heat 4 Tablespoons oil in skillet. Paint with egg wash before frying the Papas, this helps keep them from falling apart. Brown the potato and turn it carefully. Serve with rice and onion relish. Serves 8.

Onion Relish

Jenny and Koki always had a bowl of this on their counter, and they served it with everything, even scrambled eggs and rice. The lime juice essentially 'cooks' the onion so it's not raw, but it's still crunchy...delicious!

 1 cup onion (any color, chopped or sliced into rings)
 juice of 2 fresh limes
 salt, pepper

Pour lime juice over onions, toss with salt and pepper. Let sit at least one hour.
CINDY LOZA, MARION, IOWA

Papa rellena with rice, a South American treat.

FEIJOADA

This pork and black bean stew is considered by many to be Brazil's national dish. Its origins lie in the slave traditions of colonial Brazil, when slaves would put discarded cuts of meat (pig ear, snout, hock, etc.) to good use, cooking slowly over several hours. The saltiness that can come from a stew made from smoked meats is cut with the accompaniment of molho apiamento, a salsa-like sauce that adds a freshness to the dish. It is delicious served over rice.

    1 1/2 pounds smoked pork or ham hock
    1/2 package thick-cut bacon, cut in 1 inch pieces
    1 onion, chopped
    3 cloves garlic, chopped
    2 19-ounce cans black beans, drained and rinsed well
    1 cup canned crushed tomatoes
    1/4 pound ground pork, browned and drained
    1/2 pound Brazilian linguica sausage, cooked (any other cooked sausage will
    work)
    5 cups water
    Molho Apimentado (see below)

Place drained beans in a crockpot and mash slightly with a potato masher (this will help thicken the stew).

Place hock in a large stockpot filled with water, and bring to a boil to soften it up and remove impurities. Remove hock and place in crockpot with beans.

In large sauté pan, brown bacon, and drain fat, reserving one tablespoon. Add onion and garlic and sauté with bacon until soft. Add to crock pot, along with beans, tomatoes, ground pork, sausage and water. Cook on low for 2-8 hours. Serve over hot rice and top with molho apimentado.

MOLHO APIMENTADO

Very similar to fresh salsa or pico de gallo, but smaller sized pieces. If you like your sauces spicy, you can add a couple seeded, diced malagueta peppers to the mix.

 4 tomatoes, seeded and finely diced
 1 green pepper, finely diced
 1 onion, finely diced
 1/4 cup finely chopped fresh cilantro
 2 Tablespoons olive oil
 1 teaspoon vinegar
 1/2 teaspoon Kosher salt

Stir together and serve with feijoada.

VITAMINA DE ABACATE

This avocado smoothie is really simple- it's very common to see in Brasil and the funny thing is they only eat avocadoes sweet there, never salty.

 1 whole avocado
 about one cup of milk (depending on the size of the avocado, you can adjust for the right consistency)
 sugar or honey to taste

Blend together in a blender and serve.
 PORTIA BOSS, MIAMI, FLORIDA

A Word on Heifer International

PHILANTHROPY IS COMMENDABLE, BUT IT MUST NOT CAUSE
THE PHILANTHROPIST TO OVERLOOK THE CIRCUMSTANCES OF
ECONOMIC INJUSTICE WHICH MAKE PHILANTHROPY NECESSARY.

Rev. Martin Luther King, Jr.

I first heard of Heifer International when I was hanging out at my parents' house. My mother is a Christmas season catalogue addict: back in the day, her countertops and bookshelves would be covered in brightly colored magazines, offering the latest, trendiest gifts for Christmas. Flipping through these was a bit of a guilty pleasure: I refuse to receive these for environmental reasons, but I sure do love flipping through them at Mom's house. One of the ones I picked up said on the cover "The Most Important Gift Catalog in the World." *Well, that's a pretty bold statement,* I thought, and picked it up. Leafing through the Heifer Christmas catalog, I learned that this organization provided livestock and other support to families trying to make a living from subsistence or small-scale farming. A light went on and I just thought, "of course, this makes so much sense!" From that point on, Adam and I have given to Heifer in one way or another, either by mailing in checks, telling others about their programs or by hosting dinner parties as fundraisers. Eighty percent of the profits from this cookbook will go to Heifer International.

Heifer International recently released a press statement regarding the current global food crisis, and how Heifer's approach supports long-term solutions to global hunger and poverty. I have reprinted a portion of the press release here, but I urge you to visit Heifer's website, www.heifer.org, to learn more about programs that are making lasting, positive changes.

East Africa Dairy Development

"Scaling up Heifer's approach is the goal of a recent $42.8 million grant by the Bill & Melinda Gates Foundation to Heifer to expand its model to produce milk for commercial dairies in parts of Rwanda, Uganda and Kenya. The goal of the East Africa Dairy Development Project (EADD) is to help one million people – 179,000 families – lift themselves out of poverty by developing 30 milk collection hubs with "chilling plants" where farmers will bring raw milk for pickup by commercial dairies.

Heifer will organize farmer business associations to own and manage the chilling plants. Milk production will be increased through artificial insemination to improve local breeds of dairy cows and through improved animal nutrition. The project will provide extensive training in animal agriculture, business practices and other subjects.

Thus, farmers with only one or two cows will be able to participate in the "value chain" of profit through the commercial dairy industry while maintaining pastoral production methods that are environmentally friendly.

The role of relief aid

Heifer applauds and supports the vital work of disaster relief organizations. However, in times of crisis, it's important to understand the distinction between relief and sustainable development.

Ever since Heifer's founder, Dan West, came up with the phrase "not a cup, but a cow," in 1944, Heifer's approach to providing global assistance to struggling communities has been characterized by long-term development, rather than short-term relief.

As writer Cal Thomas recently stated, "One doesn't 'tackle poverty,' like a football player. One shows the way of escape and provides sufficient role models along with capital and moral and educational structures that serve as ladders so people who want to climb out of the hole can do so." Heifer couldn't agree more. It's what the organization has been doing since 1944.

About Heifer International

Heifer's mission is to end hunger and poverty while caring for the earth. For more than 60 years, Heifer International has provided livestock and environmentally sound agricultural training to improve the lives of those who struggle daily for reliable sources of food and income. Heifer is currently working in more than 57 countries, including the U.S., to help families and communities become more self-reliant. Every gift of an animal provides benefits such as milk, eggs, wool and fertilizer, increasing family incomes for better housing, nutrition, health care and school fees for children.

Recipients "Pass on the Gift" of offspring of their cows, goats and other livestock to others in an ever-widening circle of hope.

For more information, visit www.heifer.org."

Recipe Index

Bibliography

Behnke, Alison, *Cooking the Central American Way*. 2005, Lerner Publications Company, Minneapolis.

Collingham, Lizzie, *Curry: A Tale of Cooks and Conquerors*. 2006, Oxford University Press, Inc., New York.

Cummings, Joe, *World Food Thailand*. 2000, Lonely Planet Pty Ltd, Victoria, Australia.

Cornell, Kari, *Cooking the Southern African Way*. 2005, Lerner Publications Company, Minneapolis.

Del Conte, Anna, *Gastronomy of Italy*. 2001, Pavilion Books Limited, London.

Duncan, Dorothy, *Canadians at Table: A Culinary History of Canada*. 2006, Dundurn Press, Toronto.

Fallon, Steve and Michael Rothschild, *World Food France*. 2000, Lonely Planet Publications Pty Ltd, London.

Geddes, Bruce, *World Food Caribbean*. 2001, Lonely Planet Publications Pty Ltd, London.

Harris, Jessica, *The Africa Cookbook: Tastes of a Continent*. 1998, Simon & Schuster, New York.

Hirigoyen, Gerald, *The Basque Kitchen: Tempting Food from the Pyrenees*. 1999, HarperCollins Publishers, Inc., New York.

McNamee, Gregory, *Moveable Feasts: The History, Science, and Lore of Food*. 2007, Praeger Publishers, Westport.

Murray, Sarah, *Moveable Feasts: From Ancient Rome to the 21st Century, the Incredible Journeys of the Food We Eat*. 2007, St. Martin's Press, New York.

Ostmann, Barbara Gibbs and Jane L. Baker, *The Recipe Writer's Handbook*. 2001, John Wiley & Sons, Inc., New York.

Pathak, Jyoti, *Taste of Nepal*. 2007, Hippocrene Books, Inc., New York.

Sterling, Richard, Georgia Dacakis, Kate Reeves and John Burke, *World Food Greece*. 2002, Lonely Planet Publications Pty Ltd, London.

Sterling, Richard, *World Food Spain*. 2000, Lonely Planet Publications Pty Ltd, London.

Valent, Dani, *World Food Turkey*. 2000, Lonely Planet Publications Pty Ltd, London.

Witton, Patrick, *World Food Indonesia*. 2002, Lonely Planet Publications Pty Ltd, London.

Zibart, Eve. *The Ethnic Food Lover's Companion: Understanding the Cuisines of the World*. 2001, Menasha Ridge Press, Birmingham, Alabama.

ISBN 142518610-6